Edward Douglass White Lectures

THE PASSIVE JUDICIARY

THE PASSIVE JUDICIARY

PROSECUTORIAL DISCRETION AND THE GUILTY PLEA

Abraham S. Goldstein

Louisiana State University Press
Baton Rouge and London

Manufactured in the United States of America

Designer: Patricia Douglas Crowder
Typeface: L/202 Trump
Typesetter: G&S Typesetters, Inc.

LIBRARY OF CONGRESS CATALOGING IN PUBLICATION DATA

Goldstein, Abraham S.
The passive judiciary.

(Edward Douglass White lectures)
Based on the Edward Douglass White lectures, delivered at Louisiana State University, Baton Rouge, March 1977.
Includes bibliographical references and index.
1. Prosecution—United States—Decision making. 2. Pleas of guilty—United States. I. Title. II. Series.

KF9640.G64 345.73'05042 81-11749
ISBN 0-8071-0856-1 347.3055042 AACR2

For Ruth

CONTENTS

Preface and Acknowledgments xi

Introduction 3

I. CHARGING, DISMISSALS, AND INFORMAL IMMUNITY 9

A. *Nolle Prosequi* and Dismissals 12

B. Conferring Immunity from Prosecution 25

II. THE GUILTY PLEA 33

A. Legitimating the Plea Bargain 35

B. Voluntariness and Accuracy 39

C. The Judge's Discretion 47

III. A COMMON LAW OF PROSECUTORIAL DISCRETION 52

A. The Problem of Separation of Powers 53

B. Building a Common Law: Some Illustrations 58

C. A More Active Role for the Judge 67

D. A Role for the Victim 70

Notes 77

Index 101

PREFACE AND ACKNOWLEDGMENTS

This book is based upon the Edward Douglass White Lectures, delivered at Louisiana State University in Baton Rouge, Louisiana, in March, 1977. I am deeply grateful to the university, and particularly to the dean and faculty of the Law School, for inviting me to present the lectures. In the course of preparing them for publication, I have tried to avoid the temptation to convert lectures into treatise. My hope has been to retain the speculative quality of the original while adding somewhat greater detail than is appropriate to an oral presentation.

I should like to express my appreciation to the National Science Foundation, which supported some of the research upon which this book is based; to several former students of Yale Law School—Richard Hill, Walter Laughlin, Martin Marcus, and James O'Neill—for their research assistance; to my secretary, Geraldine Perillo, for her invaluable aid during the entire period of research and writing; and to many colleagues who made useful comments on an earlier draft of the manuscript: Professors Mirjan Damaska, Steven Duke, Daniel Freed, Joseph Goldstein, Barbara Underwood, and Stanton Wheeler of Yale Law School, Professor Albert Reiss of Yale's Department of Sociology, and Professor Milton Heumann of the Political Science Department, University of Michigan.

THE PASSIVE JUDICIARY

INTRODUCTION

The public prosecutor is the central figure in the administration of American criminal justice. It is he who chooses, from a mass of overlapping and redundant criminal statutes, which of them best fits the facts presented by the police. And he is the one who decides how many offenses to charge and whether the evidence will support a conviction. In making these decisions, he acts not only on "legal" grounds but on equitable and practical ones as well. He may conclude that certain statutes should not be enforced at all or that restitution to the victim suffices or that a conviction would serve no useful correctional purpose. He may even exercise a species of pardoning power, as when a charge is reduced below what the facts would establish, when immunity is conferred in return for cooperation by the suspect in the government's investigation of others, or when federal and state prosecutors decide that criminal charges should be brought in only one of the two systems. In short, the prosecutor establishes enforcement priorities and accommodates conflicting statutory, correctional, and constitutional objectives. At the same time, he individualizes justice, induces cooperation, and mitigates the severity of the criminal law. His instruments for achieving these remarkably diverse objectives are his exclusive authority to initiate a criminal charge, his power to dismiss or reduce charges, and his overwhelmingly dominant role in plea bargaining.[1]

These instruments are particularly effective because the local prosecutor enjoys an unusual degree of independence —both from administrative superiors and from judges. He is part of a criminal justice system that is remarkably decentralized and fragmented. In most states, he has no "superiors." He is elected county by county and is sufficiently autonomous so that it is incorrect to speak even of fifty "state" systems. Though the federal government is hierarchical—with the attorney general heading a Department of Justice—local United States attorneys ordinarily receive only nominal direction and review.[2] Even more fundamentally, independence comes naturally in a system, still rooted in the English tradition of private prosecution, which assumes that judges will play a reactive role and that initiatives will be left to the parties, one of whom is the public prosecutor.[3]

Judges have reinforced the prosecutor's independence by allowing him a degree of "discretion" that contrasts dramatically with the control they have exercised over official action much less familiar to them. When victims have tried to compel prosecution, on the ground that the district attorney was their surrogate and was neglecting their and the public's interest, the courts have said the victims lack "standing." They have taken the position that only the "lawyer for the people" may vindicate the public interest in criminal law enforcement. When statutes or court rules require judicial approval for dismissing or reducing the charge or accepting a guilty plea, matters have generally been left to the prosecutor. The tone has been less one of judicial restraint than of judicial withdrawal, treating the prosecutor as so integral and expert a part of the executive branch that he may not be interfered with by the judiciary.

In this setting, the courts seem almost to have forgotten principles of legality which they have enforced energetically elsewhere in the criminal law—principles that make the legislature the primary source of law and the judiciary its authoritative interpreter. The most important of these is legislative supremacy in defining what is crime and in fixing the sanction to be imposed upon conviction. It is now a commonplace, affirmed by the judiciary, that statutes must provide fair warning to potential lawbreakers, guide judges and lawyers as to what is properly in issue at trial, and put the police and prosecutors on notice as to the limits of their authority. No one, not even a judge, may declare a criminal statute "abandoned" by nonenforcement.[4] In the investigative area, too—search, interrogation, surveillance, and eavesdropping—judges have used the lever of the exclusionary rules to make it plain that they are the ultimate guardians of legality. And in these and other matters arising at trial and appeal, they have been less willing than in earlier times to leave justice entirely to the parties; they have enforced judicial conceptions of legality through the doctrine of plain error and a growing constitutional law on ineffective assistance of counsel.[5] The underlying approach is reflected in *Young* v. *United States*, in which the Supreme Court—refusing to treat the government's confession of error as determinative of whether a criminal prosecution should be terminated—said: "Such a confession of error, does not relieve this Court of the performance of the judicial function. . . . Our judicial obligations compel us to examine independently the errors confessed. . . . The public interest that a result be reached which promotes a well-ordered society is foremost in every criminal proceeding. That interest is entrusted to our consideration and protection as well as to that of the enforcing officers. Furthermore, our judgments are precedents, and the proper administration of the criminal law cannot be left merely to the stipulation of the parties."[6]

It was to be expected that the prosecutor's virtual insulation from judicial review would soon come to an end, not only because of trends already at work in the criminal law but also because the courts' attitude towards him was so much at odds with the "imperial" approach they were taking elsewhere. Courts that were integrating schools, apportioning legislatures, and determining the adequacy of prisons and mental hospitals—assuming in each instance that only the judge is "neutral and detached" enough to speak authoritatively for the rule of law—were bound eventually to turn a critical eye to the prosecutor.[7] Not only had it been made apparent by a generation of field research that his decisions often determine the meaning and effect of criminal law, but those decisions, unlike the allegedly "imperial" ones, were integral to the judge's function and to the day-to-day administration of the criminal courts.

It remained, however, for these varied elements to come into focus. This is at last occurring as part of a belated effort to bring plea bargaining under judicial control. Courts are now seeing, as if for the first time, that the prosecutor is not really a "quasi-judicial" guardian of the public interest; he is an administrative official caught up in conflicting roles. While investigating crime and prosecuting cases, he is expected to display partisan zeal and practice vigorous advocacy. Yet unlike a "mere adversary," he is expected to conform to constitutional standards and to protect the public interest.[8] In two opinions of great potential significance, the Supreme Court has recognized that it may not be possible to reconcile the conflicting roles. In *Coolidge* v. *New Hampshire,* the Court said the prosecutor is too engaged in the "competitive enterprise of ferreting out crime" to pass on the sufficiency of a search warrant in a case being investigated under his supervision. Only a judge is "neutral and impartial" enough to do so.[9] And in *Gerstein* v. *Pugh*, the Court held that an information drafted by a prosecutor is no longer regarded as "judicial" enough to provide an objective guarantee of probable cause comparable to that furnished by a grand jury, because he is inherently partisan, while it is an arm of the court.[10] In short, the prosecutor cannot be viewed as playing a judicial role—not because he is personally partisan but because he is unavoidably made partisan by his role.

In the chapters that follow, I shall consider how the prosecutor's roles are at last being teased apart in cases dealing with dismissals, guilty pleas, and discriminatory prosecution, which call into question the acquiescence of judges in the prosecutor's domination of criminal justice. I shall show that the issues now arising between judge and prosecutor replicate earlier contests between them from which the prosecutor emerged virtually unscathed. The most important of these is reflected in the stunted history of limits on the charging power itself, in the statutory efforts to bring the writ of *nolle prosequi* under judicial control, and in the curious coexistence of statutory and informal immunity procedures. I shall then turn to the belated recognition of plea bargaining and examine its effect on judicial supervision of the guilty plea. Finally, I shall question the reliance placed by the courts on the doctrine of separation of powers and shall suggest that judges should use their authority more aggressively at hearings on dismissals, charge reductions, and guilty pleas in order to build a common law of prosecutorial discretion.

I. CHARGING, DISMISSALS, AND INFORMAL IMMUNITY

A typical statute defining the authority of the district attorney provides that he "shall prosecute for all offenses" within his district. Though the language is mandatory, it has been construed as conferring on him the exclusive authority to prosecute, but not the obligation to do so in all cases.[1] He is said to have inherited from the attorney general of England an unreviewable discretion to charge or not, as he sees fit. Yet the matter is more complicated. As a public official, the prosecutor is governed by the rule of law—by the Constitution, statutes, and judicial opinions. His discretion to charge is itself a part of the authority with which he has been endowed by legislatures and courts. And some limits on that discretion, beyond those enforced by the prosecutor's own conscience, have been recognized by the courts.

In several states, a prosecutor who fails entirely to enforce a criminal law is guilty of the offense of criminal nonfeasance.[2] Under federal law, there is some support for the view that he may violate the Civil Rights Acts if he follows a policy of refusing to prosecute whites for assaults on blacks and that he may be compelled to reverse the policy.[3] It has even been suggested by two influential courts that the usual rule which denies "standing" to victims to compel prosecution might have to give way if nonenforcement is widespread enough or if it might lead to direct personal injury.[4] The most powerful limitation, however, is the rule established by the Supreme Court a century ago in *Yick Wo* v. *Hopkins*, which held that a defendant is denied equal protection under the Fourteenth Amendment if a criminal law "fair on its face and impartial in appearance . . . is applied and administered by public authority with an evil eye and an unequal hand, so as practically to make unjust and illegal discrimination between persons in similar circumstances material to their rights."[5] Revived by the Court in *Oyler* v. *Boles* after a quiescent history, this defense of "discriminatory prosecution" treats a decision to prosecute as a denial of equal protection if it is "deliberately based upon an unjustifiable standard such as race, religion, or other arbitrary classification."[6]

These separate lines of cases affirm norms of legality in charging crime, but they do so for situations that are not likely often to come to the attention of the courts. Prosecutions for criminal nonfeasance are rare, both because they require total nonenforcement of a category of crime and because prosecutors are obviously reluctant to prosecute themselves or their predecessors. Suits under the Civil Rights Acts and under the new "standing" theories also require total nonenforcement. And the defense of discriminatory prosecution requires a proof that few defendants will have either the tenacity or the resources to establish. For example, Oyler was denied relief because his allegations were insufficient to show that the disparate treatment he received was "intentional"; he had not alleged that the prosecutor knew of other offenders who, like him, had three prior convictions.[7] "All that need be shown" to defeat the claim, said the Minnesota Supreme Court when a female prostitute alleged sex discrimination in failing to prosecute male customers, is "some rational relationship between the city's objective of controlling prostitution and the practice of arresting chiefly women violators."[8] Apart from minor offenses, the claim of discriminatory prosecution has been successful only in a few cases involving the First Amendment.[9] And the most conspicuous of them, *United States* v. *Falk*, would be difficult to replicate. Falk had the extraordinary good fortune to be able to show that he had been prosecuted for violating the Selective Service Act because he was an active opponent of the draft and the Vietnam War, that the prosecution against him ran counter to a policy of nonenforcement for similar offenses embodied in a statement by the director of Selective Service, and that over 25,000 other registrants had violated the relevant statutory requirements without being prosecuted.[10] Comparable materials are rarely available to a defendant, either because they do not exist or because access to the prosecutor's files is ordinarily barred.[11]

The prosecutor's authority to charge is not so much unlimited, therefore, as it is limited by norms of equality and rationality that are difficult to enforce in the courts. These norms have remained largely latent, unless the prosecutor chooses to abide by them, even when the charge comes under judicial scrutiny on motions to dismiss or reduce the charge or to accept a guilty plea. This insulation from judicial review, which first occurred under the aegis of the writ of *nolle prosequi*, has persisted even when explicit efforts have been made to bring the charge, or the decision to confer immunity, under some species of judicial control.

A. *Nolle Prosequi* and Dismissals

The concept of an expansive prosecutorial discretion traces to a body of law that dealt not with the initiation of a charge by the prosecutor but with its termination by filing a writ of *nolle prosequi*. Upon receipt of the writ, the prosecution was ended without any inquiry by the court. The writ, and the practice, had existed in England since the sixteenth century, but there it was the attorney general who could file it, and he did so in the exercise of a reviewing authority over the private prosecutor. He used it to intervene and dismiss charges if they were frivolous or insubstantial or might somehow interfere with a crown prosecution. "[P]roceedings instituted in the name of the Crown," it was said, "should be subject to termination at the will of the Crown."[12] Private prosecution disappeared in the United States, and the local district attorney was given a monopoly of the power to prosecute, but the *nolle* remained with him, on the assumption that he had inherited the prerogatives of the attorney general of England. Through it, he was able to "dispose of criminal cases without trial and without review on grounds nowhere recorded and quite unascertainable."[13]

The earliest American opinion on the subject is *Commonwealth* v. *Wheeler*, decided in 1806. Chief Justice Theophilus Parsons noted that "[t]he power of entering a *nolle prosequi* is to be exercised at the discretion of the attorney who prosecutes for the government, and for its exercise he alone is responsible." The court, he said, is "not legally competent to give any advice" to the prosecutor on the subject.[14] More than sixty years later, in the *Confiscation Cases*, the United States Supreme Court echoed the theme. "[P]ublic prosecutions, until they come before the court . . .

are within the exclusive direction of the district attorney, and even after they are entered in court, they are so far under his control that he may enter a *nolle prosequi* at any time before the jury is empanelled for the trial of the case."[15] Even as a rule of unreviewable discretion was being established, however, it was being qualified.[16] The Supreme Court noted that it might be "otherwise provided" by Congress. A New Hampshire court said in 1875 that permission to enter a *nolle* might be refused by a judge in an "extreme case," such as one in which the prosecutor was acting corruptly.[17] Statements of deference were gradually joined with assertions that courts would interfere with prosecutorial discretion if the power "were oppressively used."[18]

The use of the *nolle* attracted little attention until the early part of the twentieth century. "Political responsibility was a check on the prosecutor in a proper sense in pioneer America, where dockets were small, where the citizens in large and representative numbers attended all trials, where everyone knew what the prosecutor did and how and why."[19] But by 1913, Judge William Gemmill decried a system under which "the public can never know whether the influences, and the motives which led to these dismissals before trial, were good or evil. . . . [T]he public is justified in its suspicion that justice, being proverbially blind, has often been sorely cheated."[20] Several years later, the Supreme Court of Illinois referred to "[t]he disastrous consequences of endowing a state's attorney with absolute and unlimited power to enter a nolle prosequi in all prosecutions of a certain class of crimes and leaving the people to the remedy of a prosecution against him for malfeasance in office."[21] In 1930, Roscoe Pound found that "the number of prosecutions . . . has become enormous—far beyond possibilities of trial. . . . [T]he common-law unlimited power of *nol. pros.* becomes a means of selection of those to be prosecuted, of which politicians have not been slow to take advantage. Originally, this was a public check upon private prosecutions. Now, it is . . . a power needing check."[22]

By 1930, the trend had shifted dramatically. Thirty-one states had adopted some form of judicial control of the *nolle*, responding to a widely held feeling that crimes should be routinely prosecuted, the dismissal power should be "seldom exercised," and that courts should interfere if the power "were oppressively used."[23] But the new statutes and rules, which required prosecutors to move for dismissal and authorized courts to grant or deny the motion, had remarkably little impact. The motion to dismiss and its corollary, the substitution of a lesser charge, were used by prosecutors as they had used the *nolle*—as if it belonged to them alone. Though they were sometimes said by statute or rule to have to justify their decisions, the courts did not often ask for explanations, or examine carefully those that were given. Motions were routinely approved and dismissals were supervised hardly at all. On the rare occasions when such matters reached the appellate courts, it was apparent that the references to review for "abuse of discretion" were little more than gestures acknowledging the reform movement. The practical effect was to restore the *status quo ante*. The prosecutor would be permitted to individualize justice as he chose, and the trial judge was expected to accept his motions to dismiss or to reduce charges.

Even where legislatures conferred upon the courts themselves the power to dismiss in "furtherance of justice" without the prosecutor having to take the initiative, as in California, judges have begun to return control to the prosecutor. The California experience is particularly instructive because the statute could not have been more explicit in trying to shift authority to the judge. The first California legislature, drawing on the inquisitorial elements in its Spanish history, abolished the *nolle prosequi* and gave the court exclusive authority to dismiss a criminal case. It could do so "either of its own motion or upon the application of the prosecuting attorney, and in furtherance of justice. . . . The reasons for the dismissal must be set forth in an order entered upon the minutes." The judge's power to dismiss was described as "substantially the same as that held by the attorney general in England, and by the prosecuting officer in many of the American states, to enter a *nolle prosequi*. The court, for the purposes of the order of dismissal, takes charge of the prosecution, and acts for the people."[24]

The judge's authority was especially apparent in cases dealing with a practice known as "striking the priors." In most jurisdictions, prosecutors may omit from the charge the allegations that would support the recidivist penalty. In California, however, counsel must ask the court, at sentencing, to "strike the prior conviction" of a defendant in order to avoid the increased sentence that would otherwise be mandatory under recidivist statutes. When the legislature tried to make the judge's authority to "strike the priors" turn on the prosecutor's concurrence, the California court found it an unconstitutional invasion of the principle of separation of powers. "The judicial power is compromised," said the court, "when a judge, who believes that a charge should be dismissed in the interests of justice, wishes to exercise the power to dismiss but finds that before he may do so he must bargain with the prosecutor."[25] In subsequent cases, the court has broadened the point, making the touchstone the filing of a criminal charge. Once that executive act is completed, the subsequent process "which leads to acquittal or to sentencing is fundamentally judicial in nature. . . . [S]eparation of powers mandates that a statute may not constitutionally require the consent of the prosecuting attorney to judicial action . . . determining that a charged offense should be tried as a misdemeanor rather than a felony . . . civilly committing a defendant to a narcotics rehabilitation program . . . or ordering a defendant charged with a narcotics offense to be 'diverted' into a pretrial program of treatment and rehabilitation."[26]

Despite the breadth of these pronouncements, there have been opinions indicating reluctance to allow the trial judge to exercise the dismissal authority too broadly. For example, when the trial judge ordered dismissal of a felony manslaughter charge because the preliminary hearing showed that the defendant had used no more force than was necessary to prevent the commission of a felony, the California Supreme Court concluded that it was wrong for the trial judge to dismiss on his own motion. "Under the adversary nature of our criminal procedure, the prosecuting attorney, as the People's representative," is in the best position to make application for a dismissal "in furtherance of justice."[27] And when a trial judge ignored the prosecutor's objection and dismissed a case in which there was probable cause of guilt, he was held to have abused his discretion.[28] The most dramatic indication of a changing mood is the sharply divided *en banc* opinion in *People* v. *Tanner*. The trial judge had stricken a jury finding that the defendant had used a firearm during commission of a robbery. Otherwise, he would have been required to deny probation, which he regarded as the appropriate sentence. A plurality of the court held that the statute making imprisonment mandatory under such circumstances was binding on the courts, overriding their discretion to dismiss or to strike allegations relevant to punishment. "We reject any contention," the court said, "that courts are inherently or constitutionally vested with ultimate authority in fixing sentences or imposing penalty enhancing factors for conduct made criminal by legislative enactment."[29] In limiting the trial judge's authority, the court affirmed a principle of *legislative* supremacy over the judiciary on the question of penalty, without considering whether the mandatory quality of the legislative provision means that the prosecutor, too, may not eliminate the firearm allegation in order to achieve probation. Nevertheless, the practical effect of the decision is to make the prosecutor's charging decision the determinative factor in granting or denying probation.

As California moves from judicial control of dismissal towards according the prosecutor somewhat greater latitude, other courts are beginning to see the need for a larger judicial role. The federal experience illustrates the trend. The early federal practice had permitted prosecutors to dismiss without court approval by filing a *nolle.* Court review was theoretically available only for "the failure of the District Attorney to exercise discretion"—that is, only if he was guilty of "corruption or malfeasance in office."[30] The Advisory Committee on the Federal Rules of Criminal Procedure recommended continuing this authority in the United States attorney but requiring that he file with the court a statement of reasons for dismissal. The recommendation was rejected and Rule 48(a) was adopted instead. Like most of the state statutes, it provided that "the Attorney General or the United States Attorney may, by leave of court, dismiss an indictment, information, or complaint." And it provided no criteria for the court's decision.[31]

In the years since adoption of the rule, few opinions have dealt with the matter, but they have uniformly held that the United States attorney does not have carte blanche. In *United States* v. *Doe*, the government moved to dismiss an indictment for tax fraud without providing any reasons to justify the dismissal. Judge Carroll Hincks held that he was entitled to be informed of the facts underlying the motion, because "the rule contemplates that the court shall exercise a sound discretion. . . . [A]t least in the absence of very exceptional circumstances, as for instance where the defendant has received a substantial sentence for another phase of the same offense, the court may not properly approve a dismissal of the entire case against any given defendant unless satisfied that the government lacks sufficient evidence to warrant a prosecution. Especially is this so where the matter is before the court on indictment as distinguished from information." He noted, however, that the court would not prevent the dismissal of fewer than all the counts, pursuant to a plea bargain between the parties, as long as the court was left with "ample discretion in fixing a sentence deemed fully to satisfy the ends of justice."[32]

United States v. *Shanahan* took a similar position on similar facts. The United States attorney had moved to dismiss a perjury indictment without informing the court of the reasons for his request. The court made it clear that "it is for the court . . . to agree or disagree with the conclusion of the Attorney General or the United States Attorney that the dismissal is 'in the interests of justice.'" But it could not discharge its responsibility unless it first obtained from the government "explanatory facts" justifying the dismissal: "How can any judge exercise the sound judicial discretion with which he is charged under Rule 48(a) when he is given absolutely no factual basis upon which to base such discretion? The answer is apparent, he cannot." Upon being told that failure to dismiss would prejudice the prosecution of "another and more far reaching criminal action," the court found the reason adequate and approved the dismissal.[33]

In *United States* v. *Greater Blouse*, Judge Edward Weinfeld agreed that "public exposure of the reasons for the abandonment of" a prosecution was essential in order "to prevent abuse of the uncontrolled power of dismissal previously enjoyed by prosecutors." There would be no purpose to the rule if the prosecutor's motion were treated as "conclusive upon the Court." He noted, however, that the prosecutor's motion was "entitled to great weight" and should be granted when "the Government is without sufficient evidence to warrant prosecution and sustain a conviction," and when "the dismissal is not for the purpose of subjecting a defendant to harassment by the commencement of another prosecution at a different time or at a place deemed more favorable to the prosecution." The motion should be denied only if it "clearly and convincingly appear[s] that the public interest requires its refusal."[34]

Judge Weinfeld then took the issue a constitutional step further. He posed a question that was interesting, provocative, and entirely unnecessary (since he had consented to the dismissal): "Should the motion be denied, what next?" His answer was an amalgam of practical considerations and the constitutional doctrine of separation of powers. In his words:

> The Attorney General is the head of the Department of Justice, a part of the Executive branch of Government. Even were leave of Court to the dismissal of the indictment denied, the Attorney General would still have the right to adhere to the Department's view that the indictment cannot be supported by proof upon a trial of the merits, and accordingly, in the exercise of his discretion, decline to move the case for trial. The Court in that circumstance would be without power to issue a mandamus or other order to compel prosecution of the indictment, since such a direction would invade the traditional separation of powers doctrine. And if the indictment continues to remain in status quo, each defendant would be in a position to move for dismissal of the indictment . . . [for failure of prosecution]. While this does not nullify the responsibility of the Court where its sanction is being sought, it is a factor to be taken into account.[35]

Though Judge Weinfeld was writing about an indictment that could "not be supported by proof" at trial, his words have been taken to mean that judicial review of dismissals is destined to be ineffective because a federal judge is barred by constitutional law from examining the details of the charging process. He has been understood as suggesting there may be nothing a judge can do even if the prosecutor's reasons for dismissal are patently unsatisfactory. Charles Wright, and the draftsmen of the new *Uniform Rules of Criminal Procedure,* have pressed the view to its seemingly logical conclusion. They recommend abandoning a requirement of judicial approval because, in Wright's words, "The court is powerless to compel a prosecutor to proceed in a case which he believes does not warrant prosecution."[36] They would take us back to the point at which the American law of *nolle prosequi* began—with the prosecutor vested with an absolute and unreviewable power to dismiss a charge.

Despite the apparent centrality of the constitutional issues, they received surprisingly little attention until *United States* v. *Cox*. *Cox* grew out of an indictment returned by a federal grand jury in Mississippi against several civil rights workers. Under Federal Rule 6, a prosecution may not go forward unless either the United States attorney or the attorney general signs the indictment. In this instance, both refused to do so. District Judge Harold Cox held the United States attorney in contempt for his refusal. His decision was reversed by the Fifth Circuit, which said that the power to control the initiation of a criminal charge by "affixing or withholding . . . the signature is a matter of executive discretion which cannot be coerced or reviewed by the courts." In the course of its opinion, the court read Rule 48(a) as designed solely to protect a defendant from the harassment of multiple prosecutions. It rejected the argument that the rule, which authorizes dismissals only "by leave of court," signified a general authority in the judge to supervise the prosecutor's discretion. Judicial review of the power to *initiate* a charge, it noted, might cast doubt on the constitutional validity of the rule: "[M]atters of policy wholly apart from any question of probable cause" are inevitably caught up in the prosecutor's decision to charge. "[A]s an incident of the constitutional separation of powers . . . the courts are not to interfere with the free exercise of the discretionary powers of the attorneys of the United States in their control over criminal prosecutions."[37]

The dissenting judges regarded the signature requirement as ministerial and as incidental to the constitutional powers of a grand jury. When an indictment was returned, prosecutors were obligated to go forward with it unless they could persuade a judge to dismiss under Rule 48: "The court, in the interest of justice, may require a showing of good faith [by the prosecutor], and a statement of some rational basis for dismissal. In the unlikely event of bad faith or irrational action . . . it may be that the court could appoint court counsel to prosecute the case. In brief, the court may have the same inherent power to administer justice to the government as it does to the defendant."[38]

The issues were explored again by the same court in *United States* v. *Cowan*, a case involving dismissal as part of a "plea bargain." The United States attorney had moved to dismiss all federal charges pending against Jake Jacobsen in Texas for bank fraud and for perjury. In return, Jacobsen had agreed to plead guilty in the District of Columbia to one count of a bribery charge pending against him and John Connally, and to testify as a government witness against Connally. Judge Robert Hill denied the motion to dismiss the Texas case. Holding that he was obligated under Rule 48 to determine if the dismissal was compatible with the public interest as well as the defendant's, he ruled there was no "factual basis" for the prosecutor's action: "[T]his court is unable to perceive how the best interest of justice could be served by dismissing serious charges with a potential penalty of 35 years imprisonment and a $70,000 fine in exchange for a guilty plea in an unrelated case carrying a maximum penalty of 2 years and a $10,000 fine. This is especially so in view of the fact that there has been *no* showing that Jacobsen's testimony is vital or essential to the successful prosecution of the District of Columbia case or any other case."[39] The Texas prosecutor then filed a statement of intention not to prosecute Jacobsen and precipitated the confrontation anticipated by Judge Weinfeld in *Greater Blouse*. Judge Hill did not back off. He appointed two special prosecutors to carry on the case, finding his authority in Rule 48 and in a court's "inherent power" to ensure justice. To do otherwise, he said, would be to nullify the dismissal rule and abandon "a valid existing indictment" that had been returned by a grand jury.[40]

The Fifth Circuit reversed Judge Hill. It said that there must be a "rational basis" for the dismissal but concluded that such a basis existed. "It was within the province of the two prosecutorial arms of the government to weigh the relative importance of two separate prosecutions in two districts and dispose of them as practical considerations seemed to dictate." As to the special prosecutor, there was no occasion "to consider the propriety of [Judge Hill's] order" because the case was to be dismissed. The court distinguished between the initiation of a prosecution, as to which "[t]he Executive remains the absolute judge," and termination, as to which federal judges are "clothe[d] with a discretion broad enough to protect the public interest in the fair administration of criminal justice." Even as to termination, the exercise of discretion by the executive branch "should not be judicially disturbed unless clearly contrary to manifest public interest."[41]

In the states, particularly those in which there is ordinarily no grand jury, the wall between the judge and the initiation of a prosecution is not always as high. A Nebraska statute, for example, provides that a prosecutor must file "reasons" with the court if he decides not to file an information after an arrest. If the court is not "satisfied" with his statement, "the county attorney shall be directed by the court to file the proper information and bring the case to trial."[42] A Colorado statute takes a similar course. It provides that a judge may require prosecution if, after receiving an affidavit "alleging the commission of a crime and the unjustified refusal of the prosecuting attorney to prosecute any person for the crime," and after hearing the prosecutor's explanation of his refusal, he finds that the refusal to prosecute was "arbitrary or capricious and without reasonable excuse." The judge may order the district attorney to "file an information and prosecute the case or may appoint a special prosecutor to do so."[43]

In sum, as the law of dismissals has evolved, a clear distinction is made between the dismissal of charges and the prosecutor's initial charging authority. Once a formal charge has been filed, it is the judge who makes the dismissal decision. The same is true of charge reductions, since they always involve the dismissal of one charge and the filing of another. The judge is entitled to the prosecutor's reasons and he may find them insufficient. He may deny motions to dismiss or to reduce charges when they interfere too much with his sentencing powers, or when there is ample evidence to support prosecution and no countervailing law enforcement reason for not doing so, such as the cooperation of the defendant, or when they indicate harassment by repeated prosecutions. Even "diversion," which began as a regularization of preexisting prosecutorial discretion, a species of prosecutorial probation, has been drawn increasingly under judicial scrutiny.[44] A common law of dismissals seemed well on its way to reversing the older tendency to endorse routinely the prosecutor's motions to dismiss when the separation-of-powers doctrine entered on the scene and introduced a new sense of constitutional constraint about judicial inquiry into the prosecutor's actions. I shall return to the question of separation of powers in a later chapter, after I have examined the relation between judge and prosecutor in several other contexts.

B. Conferring Immunity from Prosecution

A specialized facet of the charging power—and one that is integral to the guilty plea—is the decision not to charge, or to dismiss or reduce a charge, in order to reward or compel assistance from informers, cooperative witnesses, and co-conspirators. As early as the seventeenth century, colonial and parliamentary legislators recognized that compelling such cooperation would deprive a person of his privilege against self-incrimination unless he were assured by statute of immunity from prosecution.[45] Statutes now exist in every jurisdiction which authorize using the full force of the state, backed by the contempt power, upon a recalcitrant witness who is often also a prospective defendant.

These statutes make explicit that only the prosecutor may initiate the immunity process, but he may never act alone. He must obtain the formal concurrence of the court or of both the attorney general and the court. For example, the Model Immunity Act offers two alternatives: under the first, the court "shall" grant the order when the prosecuting attorney has obtained the attorney general's approval; under the second, for states where the attorney general plays no part in enforcing criminal law, a judge must issue the order unless it would be "clearly contrary to the public interest." But he must serve as an analogue of an attorney general in assuring accountability in the county prosecutor. In both variations, however, "the enforcement authorities" are regarded as "the agency best qualified to make the determination . . . [because they are] thoroughly and currently conversant with both the general and detailed situation regarding enforcement of the criminal laws. To make a wise decision that agency should be informed with respect to the particular witness involved, his offense, and his importance to the proceeding. It should be equipped to weigh this proceeding against others pending or planned, not merely locally but on a wider basis."[46]

The federal statute follows the first pattern. It provides that the court "shall issue" the order whenever in the "judgment" of the United States attorney, "the testimony or other information from such individual may be necessary to the public interest," if he has first obtained the approval of the attorney general.[47] The legislative committee reports emphasize that a local prosecutor is not authorized to give "immunity baths" unless he has the concurrence of the "two other independent but interested parties."[48] If the statutory procedures have been followed, judges have no discretion "to deny the order on the grounds that the public interest does not warrant it."[49] The statute's substantive language "does not address itself to the judiciary. . . . [H]aving stated their conclusion, the government's attorneys need not justify it. The court cannot review their judgment in this regard."[50]

Alongside these statutes, however, is a process of informal immunity administered by prosecutors. Some species of such immunity is conferred whenever the prosecutor decides not to charge at all or to drop or reduce charges he might have been able to prove.[51] "The typical state's witness offers no continuing value to the police or prosecutor and is usually only too happy to settle for charge and sentencing leniency that, without such cooperation, would be inappropriate in view of his past record and present involvement."[52] The courts have acquiesced in these practices by routinely granting motions to dismiss counts, indictments, or motions to sever defendants from joint trials until they have made good on their promises of cooperation, or by accepting guilty pleas to one of several counts or charges. In practice over the years, the formal immunity process has become a limited adjunct to the informal one, providing the prosecutor with the threat and the fact of imprisonment for those who will not cooperate in return for informal immunity.

Judicial acquiescence in the use of informal immunity began at a time when the practice was generally thought to be invalid. The Supreme Court held in the "Whiskey Cases," decided in 1878, that an indictment against a cooperating defendant should not be dismissed even though the defendant had testified for the government under an agreement that all other charges against him would be dropped when he pleaded guilty to a single count.[53] After reviewing the English and American cases, the Court held that "the district attorney had no authority to make the agreement." An accomplice who testifies for the state may claim only an "equitable title to be recommended to mercy" through clemency or pardon.[54] Chief Judge Benjamin Cardozo explained the position in a somewhat different context in *Doyle* v. *Hofstadter*:

> A power to suspend the criminal law by the tender of immunity is not an implied or an inherent incident of the power to investigate. It may be necessary for fruitful results in a particular instance, but it is not so generally indispensable as to attach itself automatically to the mere power to inquire. Whether the good to be attained by procuring the testimony of criminals is greater or less than the evil to be wrought by exempting them forever from prosecution for their crimes is a matter of high policy as to which the law-making department of the government is entitled to be heard.[55]

Over the years, informal immunity existed in a twilight zone. Though it was conferred often by prosecutors, it depended for its enforcement upon the good faith of the parties and upon bogus rationalizations that treated cooperation as evidence of contrition or rehabilitation in order to justify a dismissal, charge reduction, or sentencing concession. One of the few opinions that deals explicitly with the relationship between the two processes[56] is that of the California court in *People* v. *Brunner*. Mary Brunner, a member of the Charles Manson "gang," had allegedly participated in the murder of Gary Hinman. Bypassing the California immunity statute, the prosecutor offered her informal immunity in return for her testimony against Robert Beausoleil. Brunner accepted the offer and testified before the grand jury and at a later trial that resulted in conviction. Subsequently, she first recanted her trial testimony in an affidavit submitted by Beausoleil, and then testified contrary to the affidavit, which left the conviction undisturbed. Finally, when Manson was tried for the same murder, she asserted her privilege against self-incrimination. The prosecution read her prior testimony into the record and the jury brought in a verdict of guilty against Manson.

Brunner's conduct at the Manson trial was regarded by the district attorney as a breach of the informal immunity agreement. As a result, he indicted her, too, for the Hinman murder. The trial judge treated the immunity agreement as a bar to her prosecution and dismissed the indictment. On appeal, the state argued both that the statutory path to immunity was exclusive and that Brunner had breached the agreement by failing to cooperate in the second trial. The appellate court extolled the virtues of the statutory procedure, pointing out that it was "broad enough to protect the prosecutor against double-dealing and enable him to make an enforceable agreement with the most duplicitous witness. . . . [T]he bargain between prosecutor and witness, each to perform certain acts in the future, can be made a matter of record. . . . [T]he section also protects the witness against prosecution pressure to color existing, or to create additional testimony in order to obtain previously promised immunity." Moreover, the statute "enables an impartial judicial officer to review the propriety of the immunity bargain itself." It "preserves to the prosecuting authorities the principal control over grants of immunity," while leaving to the court "ample authority to prevent major abuses. The veto power [of the court serves] as a salutary check against the possible overzealousness, unwisdom, or corruption of local prosecutors." In the end, however, the court enforced the informal grant, saying:

> The People are estopped from arguing non-compliance. It would be anomalous to permit the People represented by the district attorney, to argue that an earlier agreement entered into by the district attorney was void for lack of compliance with a statute of whose existence the district attorney must have been aware. . . . [And, as to "breach"], performance can be measured, at least in part, by results. Since the People got their hoped-for results through the use of Brunner's testimony, we conclude albeit somewhat pragmatically, that enough of the bargain was kept to make it operative.[57]

United States v. *Carter* again presented the conflict between formal and informal immunity and again refused to treat the statutory procedure as exclusive. Carter had pleaded guilty to one misdemeanor count, after having been promised immunity for several related offenses. The promise was made in exchange for information supplied by him to federal officers in the District of Columbia. He was then indicted for the related offenses in the federal court in Virginia—on information obtained from independent sources—and was convicted. The United States Court of Appeals for the Fourth Circuit held that the District of Columbia agreement was a bar to the later Virginia prosecution, saying: "If there be fear that a United States attorney may unreasonably bargain away the government's right and duty to prosecute, the solution lies in the administrative controls which the Attorney General of the United States may promulgate to regulate and control the conduct of cases by the United States Attorneys and their assistants. The solution does not lie in formalisms about the express, implied or apparent authority of one United States Attorney, or his representative, to bind another United States Attorney."[58] *Carter* explicitly rejected the rule of the "Whiskey Cases" and placed heavy emphasis upon "the honor of the government, public confidence in the fair administration of justice, and the efficient administration of justice in a federal scheme of government."

Santobello v. *New York* seems at first glance to conclude the matter. Though the case involved neither a promise of immunity nor "cooperative" testimony, the Supreme Court used language broad enough to encompass the estoppel rationale in *Carter*: "When a [guilty] plea rests in any significant degree on a promise or agreement of the prosecutor, so that it can be said to be a part of the inducement or consideration, such promise must be fulfilled."[59] The opinion presaged routine enforcement of an informal grant of immunity when it is part of a plea bargain and when the *status quo ante* cannot be restored. At the same time, these cases—based as they are on notions of honor and estoppel—leave some difficult questions unanswered. Is the prosecutor authorized to promise immunity in the first instance, and under what circumstances? Do courts have a substantive role in curtailing or containing informal immunity? Should that role be different in the federal system, which is supervised by the attorney general of the United States, than in a state where the decision is made by an autonomous county attorney? May the informal procedure be used to avoid the requirements of the statutory procedure?

The answers to these questions would seem to be implicit in the very existence of the statutory procedures. When the formal process is used, the customary rule of virtual nonreview by the courts is appropriate because the legislature has specified procedures, including administrative review, to assure the substantive validity of the prosecutor's decision. Informal immunity, on the other hand, has none of these safeguards. It was for this very reason that the "hope" was expressed on the floor of the House that the federal immunity statute would bring informal immunity "out into the open," encouraging prosecutors to proceed by the statutory route.[60] It would seem, therefore, that prosecutors should be obligated to use the statutory procedure unless there are exceptional circumstances. But there remains the question whether, and when, this obligation can be enforced. When immunity is provided through the dismissal or reduction of a charge, there plainly exists an occasion for enforcing the statutory requirements, and that is the hearing on the motion to dismiss or on the guilty plea. And if the prosecutor should try to avoid judicial scrutiny by not charging at all, the courts might insist that immunity arrangements will not be enforced unless they are preceded by a formal charge; the grant of immunity would then be conferred by the court when it dismissed the charge. Such a requirement would bring all grants of immunity under judicial scrutiny and would avoid the claim of "executive prerogative" associated with original charging decisions under existing law. But even if informal immunity were to be regarded as intrinsically executive—because it is an aid to investigation, a judicial role need not be precluded. When judges issue arrest and search warrants, they are routinely involved in *ex parte* and secret relations with police and prosecutors, appraising their justifications for actions that are concededly executive and investigative in nature. It is not at all apparent why they should not play a similar role when immunity is conferred.

II.

THE GUILTY PLEA

Guilty pleas divide into three basic types. The first is entirely voluntary or uninfluenced; the defendant pleads because his culpability is so blatant that a trial would be meaningless, or to satisfy the qualms of conscience, or because he sees no advantage from denying his guilt. In the second, the "structurally induced" plea, he pleads guilty because a heavier penalty has been mandated by the legislature for those who insist on trial, or because it is generally known that judges impose more lenient sentences on persons who waive their trial rights. The third, the "negotiated" plea, involves a bargain struck before trial by prosecutor and defendant as to the charge, the sentence, or both. In all three types, everyone appears to benefit. The defendant avoids the risk of a heavier sentence than he in fact receives; his counsel obtains his fee with less effort; the prosecutor obtains a conviction without risking acquittal at trial; and the state determines guilt more economically because it is not put to its constitutional burden of proof. The only loser may be the public interest in maintaining a system of criminal justice based on complete accuracy and on constitutional procedures. Such losses are especially likely to occur in the second and third forms of plea, which depend for their success upon the defendant's waiver of his right to trial (and the issues he might raise there) and upon a party consensus as to the charge and the sentence.

Until recently, it was assumed that most influenced guilty pleas could not honestly be accepted by trial judges if the arrangements underlying them were exposed to view. They would be regarded as unlawful—either because the pleas were being coerced or because prosecutors were not authorized to compromise matters made criminal by the legislature. As a result, we had two systems of criminal justice: a fictional one in which prosecutors offered no inducements for guilty pleas, judges did not reward them, and defendants pleaded guilty only to charges accurately reflecting the facts of their criminal conduct; and a real one in which bargains were struck which served the interests of prosecutor and defendant but which did not necessarily serve the "public" interest. To maintain the fiction, prosecutors were permitted to describe cases as if there was insufficient evidence of the greater crime or not enough time to pursue the investigation, so that judges could purport to acquiesce in administrative judgments on the allocation of resources. Similarly, cooperation was treated as evidence of contrition or rehabilitation when other purposes were plainly being served. The real and the fictional worlds came into conflict and into public view only on the rare occasions when a defendant sought to withdraw his plea because a prosecutor had not kept his promise. Otherwise, the courts assumed a hands-off role after the charging decision, which was virtually identical with their role when the prosecutor decided not to charge at all.[1]

In 1970, the Supreme Court at last recognized the extent to which plea bargaining dominated the administration of criminal justice. Entering a world previously concealed from it, the Court considered as if for the first time how judges should deal with rights waived by defendants in exchange for benefits promised by prosecutors or expected from them or from judges, or with offenses forgiven or prosecutions abandoned in exchange for the defendant's plea to less than all the crimes he may have committed. In short, it began in that year to examine the issues bound up in the decisions on dismissals, charge reductions, and guilty pleas. In this chapter, I shall review the 1970 opinions and the cases dealing more generally with the judge's review of the guilty plea to see how much of a framework they provide for the relation between judge and prosecutor.

A. Legitimating the Plea Bargain

Curiously, none of the 1970 opinions considered the negotiated plea on facts squarely presenting the issue of its legitimacy. In *Brady* v. *United States*, the Court spoke approvingly of "bargaining," on the assumption that it was positively related to rehabilitation, but the case involved a structurally induced plea, not a negotiated one.[2] There was no promise by the prosecutor and no plea bargaining. The defendant was faced with a choice between a legislatively mandated death sentence (which could be imposed if he were convicted by a jury after pleading not guilty) and a maximum sentence of life imprisonment if he were to plead guilty. Neither the judge's authority nor the prosecutor's was in issue. In the court's words, the defendant was subjected to "no threats or promises in face-to-face encounters with" a prosecutor or judge.[3] Only the defendant's motivation in dealing with a legislative judgment was under consideration, and it was treated as irrelevant to the voluntariness of his plea. Similarly, in *North Carolina* v. *Alford*, there were no threats or promises by the prosecutor.[4] The plea to a charge of second-degree murder was held valid even though the defendant asserted his innocence, as long as the court found there was a "strong factual basis for the plea." The issue was the defendant's state of mind and the equivocal nature of the guilty plea, not the authority of the prosecutor.

Santobello v. *New York*, discussed earlier, did involve a plea bargain. The plea had been induced by the prosecutor's promise that he would recommend leniency. But the court relied on notions of estoppel to decide the case, thereby avoiding the issue of the prosecutor's authority. In an opinion describing plea bargaining as "an essential component of the administration of justice" that was to be "encouraged" if "properly administered," the court held that "when a plea rests in any significant degree on a promise or agreement of the prosecutor, so that it can be said to be part of the inducement or consideration, such promise must be fulfilled."[5] This estoppel approach is based on "expectations reasonably formed" in the defendant and on the "honor of the government in making and abiding by its proposals." It has even been extended by a lower court to prevent a prosecutor's vetoing a proposal—that had not yet been accepted by defense counsel—"for no other reason than that a superior disagrees with an apparently authorized subordinate's judgment in making it."[6]

These developments gained momentum without any discussion by the Supreme Court as to whether the prosecutor is *authorized* to offer immunity from prosecution, dismissal or reduction of a charge, or leniency in sentencing in order to induce a guilty plea. *Brady* made explicit how much was being left open. Quoting from the Fifth Circuit opinion in *Shelton* v. *United States*, it defined a guilty plea as involuntary if it was "induced by threats (or promises to discontinue improper harassment), misrepresentation (including unfulfilled or unfulfillable promises), or perhaps by promises that are by their nature improper as having no proper relationship to the prosecutor's business."[7] In a footnote, the court reserved the question raised by a "situation where the prosecutor or judge, or both, deliberately employ their charging and sentencing powers to induce a particular defendant to tender a plea of guilty."[8] Even as to a structurally induced plea, it cautioned, "We would have serious doubts about this case if the encouragement of guilty pleas by offers of leniency substantially increased the likelihood that defendants, advised by competent counsel, would falsely condemn themselves."[9]

Though *Brady* squarely rejected the view that "justice and liberty are not the subjects of bargaining and barter," and that a plea "induced by a promise of recommended leniency" is necessarily involuntary, it plainly contemplated a course of decisions tracing what governmental actions were sufficiently improper to warrant rejecting pleas induced by them.[10] Having abandoned the view that the only voluntary plea is one that is virtually spontaneous to the defendant, the court took the marketplace as its model. The state may make it attractive for the defendant to plead guilty in order to conserve scarce resources. But the state must be fair, and the court must ensure that there has been no "improper" inducement. The key is the defendant's willingness, with advice of counsel, to plead guilty and to suffer adverse consequences in a context of relatively moderate pressure.[11]

Bordenkircher v. *Hayes*, decided in 1978, addressed one of the key pressures involved in bargaining—the prosecutor's authority to threaten more serious charges in order to persuade a defendant to plead guilty. The defendant had been told he would be charged as a recidivist, which carries a very heavy sentence, if he did not plead guilty to forgery. When the defendant refused, the more serious charge was brought. Defendant moved to dismiss it as an invalid and vindictive use of the charging power, but the Court rejected the claim:

> In the "give-and-take" of plea bargaining, there is no . . . element of punishment or retaliation so long as the accused is free to accept or reject the prosecution's offer. . . . By hypothesis, the plea may have been induced by promises of a recommendation of a lenient sentence or a reduction of charges, and thus by fear of the possibility of a greater penalty upon conviction after a trial. . . . [By] tolerating and encouraging the negotiation of pleas, this Court has necessarily accepted as constitutionally legitimate the simple reality that the prosecutor's interest at the bargaining table is to persuade the defendant to forego his right to plead not guilty.[12]

The only limit imposed by the Court on the use of a threat to charge a more serious offense is that the prosecutor must not "bluff." He must have probable cause to believe the defendant committed the offenses that are the subject of his "threat."[13]

The legitimation of plea bargaining was completed in the federal courts, and in an increasing number of states, by the adoption of rules establishing procedures for plea discussions or negotiations and for offering a conditional plea of guilty. A new Rule 11(e) was added to the *Federal Rules of Criminal Procedure*, for example, and the Advisory Committee note heralded it as giving "recognition to the propriety of plea discussions and plea agreements provided that they are disclosed in open court and subject to acceptance or rejection by the trial judge." Generally, they authorize plea negotiations and their corollaries—reduced charges, dismissals, agreement on sentence and recommendations—and require that promises be recorded in a plea agreement.[14] Still unsettled by the Court and the rules, however, are the details: What constitutes "probable cause" for a charge and to what extent may judges ascertain whether it exists? What promises are "by their nature improper as having no proper relationship to the prosecutor's business?" What is "improper harassment?" What promises are "unfulfillable?" And how much leniency may prosecutors offer? These are left to the judge to decide case by case when he is asked to accept a guilty plea.

B. Voluntariness and Accuracy

The defendant has a right to proffer a guilty plea, but he has no right to have it accepted. The decision on acceptance is committed by law to the judge and depends on the plea's meeting three requirements: It must be voluntary, it must be accurate, and it must be consistent with the sound administration of criminal justice.

I have already noted the Supreme Court's view that structural inducements and certain inducements in the course of plea negotiations do not necessarily render a plea involuntary. And I have pointed to the many questions about an influenced plea that remain unanswered. But the uninfluenced plea, too, presents serious problems. The judge must determine that the defendant genuinely understands the nature of the charge against him, the consequences of his plea, and the defenses he may be waiving.[15] Though he looks to defense counsel to provide the requisite assurance and gives the defendant himself more explicit advice on these matters than in the past, he retains an affirmative obligation to assure that the plea is indeed voluntary.

The most elusive issue the judge faces is the degree of latitude the defendant should be allowed in waiving either insufficiencies of proof or violations of law—by the prosecutor, the police, or the jury commissioner. The defendant may well understand, for example, that he has a defense on the merits or a plausible claim that he was searched illegally, or that the grand jury which indicted him was selected in violation of the equal protection clause, or that the prosecutor used improper pressures.[16] But he may not care. His only concern may be to get the charge and/or sentence reduced to tolerable levels—perhaps because he is not confident his claims will prevail. And what he regards as tolerable may have little to do with the public interest in accuracy, deterrence, correction, or lawful searches. The inquiry into "voluntariness" often turns, therefore, on questions regarding the judge's authority to get behind what is presented to him by the parties and the extent to which he is independently responsible for the public interest in these matters.

The requirement that the plea must be accurate presents even greater difficulties. Those most commonly discussed are whether the judge must make any inquiry into the facts at all and how much he must elicit before he is satisfied that there is a factual basis for the plea. Much more puzzling, however, is the relationship that must exist between the charge pleaded to and the crime actually committed. In practice, the judge may be presented with a guilty plea to a charge less than warranted by the facts, or with a charge of one of several possible offenses. The true facts may involve rape, not indecent assault as charged; robbery, not larceny;

seven forgeries or robberies, not one. In another variant, the prosecutor may have presented an accurate "on the nose" charge or charges and then moved to dismiss and to substitute less serious or fewer offenses. The result, in a large proportion of cases, is that the crime of which the defendant stands convicted by his plea has little or no relation to what he actually did, or how often.

The federal rules illustrate the virtual abandonment of an interest in accurate pleas. Rule 11(f) bears a caption that describes its function as "Determining the Accuracy of the Plea." The rule itself, however, drops the word "accuracy" and says only that "there must be a factual basis for the plea."[17] Though "factual basis" might be read as requiring the court to find that the plea accurately reflects the underlying facts of the crime, practice is to the contrary. And the cases, though few in number and hardly authoritative, suggest that the judge's inquiry into "factual basis" is merely a part of his obligation to see to it that the plea is voluntary.[18] Under this view, the primary purpose of the inquiry is "to ensure that the defendant actually committed a crime at least as serious as the one to which he is willing to plead."[19] As long as the judge is left with adequate sentencing authority, it is said, there is no reason to intrude on the arrangements made by the parties.

This view is taken to an extreme in New York, which holds that illogical or inconsistent pleas, and pleas under circumstances in which it is clear that the defendant did not commit the precise crime to which he is pleading, furnish no basis for judicial rejection. The leading opinion is *People* v. *Griffin*, in which two counts of assault in the second degree had been charged.[20] Griffin and the assistant district attorney negotiated a plea of guilty to one count of attempt to commit assault in the second degree. After accepting the plea, the trial judge held a hearing to determine whether the defendant had been armed, a fact that subjects him to increased punishment under New York law. On finding that he had been armed, the judge added a sentence of five to ten years. The court of appeals reversed, holding that the trial court should have enforced the understanding reached by prosecutor and defendant. The court treated an unarmed assault, which was the subject of the understanding, as a "lesser" crime that could be the subject of a guilty plea even if defendant was indeed armed. There was no need, said the Court, for the plea to be made to "a lower degree of the same crime [as in the indictment] . . . [or] an included crime;" the crime confessed did not even have to reflect the true facts. "The judgment entered on the plea in such situations may be based upon no objective state of facts. It is often a hypothetical crime, and the procedure—authorized by statute—is justified for the reason that it is in substitution for a charge of crime of a more serious nature which has been charged but perhaps cannot be proved. After a plea to a lesser crime has been accepted, the factual basis of the crime confessed can ordinarily be found only in the language of the plea."[21] The court treated the benefit to the defendant from a reduction of charges as justifying his waiver of the right to be free from conviction of a crime he had not committed. It did not make clear, however, whether factually guilty persons should be punished, despite the lack of proof, or whether a completely innocent defendant should be permitted to waive his right not to be convicted. In short, the court condoned using the threat of prosecution for a charge that "perhaps cannot be proved" to induce a guilty plea for a less serious charge whose accuracy need not be appraised at all. It has gone even further, upholding a plea to the "logically impossible" crime of attempted manslaughter because it "was sought by defendant and freely taken as part of a bargain which was struck for the defendant's benefit."[22]

There are, however, limits on how much the plea may deviate from the underlying facts, though the Supreme Court has said relatively little on the subject. In *North Carolina* v. *Alford*, where a defendant asserted his innocence while pleading guilty, the court said the trial judge must find "a strong factual basis" for the offense to which he pleads.[23] And in *Bordenkircher* v. *Hayes*, the court tied the prosecutor's charging discretion to the existence of "probable cause to believe that the accused committed an offense defined by statute," which would seem to preclude both "bluff" by prosecutor and hypothetical crimes.[24] Some states have taken a procedural approach to the problem and regarded a guilty plea to grand larceny, which had not been charged and was not a lesser included offense, as a denial of due process of law.[25] Others have treated such cases as involving a permissible informal amendment of the indictment or information. But most have seen "no need to fashion such a fiction" as long as the offense is "reasonably related" to the charge.[26] Federal Rule 11(e)(1), for example, permits negotiated charge reduction to "a lesser or related offense," as does Arizona, which requires the reduced charge to bear "some categoric similarity to the original charge." The Arizona court relies heavily on an accuracy rationale, expressing a public interest in "an accurate criminal record for the defendant, and those who must deal with him in the future." In pursuit of that objective, it has rejected a plea to obtaining money by confidence game when the facts showed either embezzlement or purse-snatching, refusing to have "appellant's criminal record . . . forever reflect not a mere inaccuracy . . . [but] an outright and misleading falsehood . . . [which] would involve a fraud on the courts."[27]

Michigan has generally followed the New York position. With an occasional exception,[28] it treats the defendant as estopped from complaining of bargained reductions that work to his advantage. For example, a plea to a lesser offense will not be reversed if the judge's inquiry into the facts indicates that the defendant was guilty of the greater offense.[29] And a defendant can "not now be heard to claim that he was harmed" by a plea to a nonexistent offense ("attempted assault with intent to commit rape") that is part of a bargain.[30] "If there is any miscarriage of justice . . . it can only be one in which the People . . . have exacted an insufficient penalty."[31] Maine's approach is even more casual. Responding to a defendant's complaint that an accomplice cooperating with the government was permitted to plead to breaking and entering in the daytime while he was convicted of burglary at night, the court described the inconsistency as a "superficial" one that "does not make a mockery of the judicial system."[32] The approach of these cases is reminiscent of the "harmless error" doctrine and makes rough justice suffice in the context of a negotiated plea. The interest in accuracy is subordinated to facilitating plea bargains and encouraging cooperation with the authorities without making clear why these objectives would not be better served by judges exercising their sentencing discretion on pleas as accurate as the available facts permit.

The distorting effect of inaccurate pleas is obvious. They make the world of crime and corrections a world of fictions. The criminal conviction becomes a suspect unit of analysis for counting crimes, for sentencing, for making restitutionary awards, and for parole. Probation officers submit reports describing cases of rape or armed robbery to judges and correctional officials who are then obligated by principles of legality to treat the offenses as less than they plainly are. Officials all along the line, as well as the public, often find themselves searching for the "real" offense concealed behind the fictional plea in an attempt to restore the proper fit between the sanction and the charge. Sentences imposed by judges and parole boards may, as a result, be as great for the lesser charge as for the greater, without the defendant being aware of the fact that he has gained no advantage by his plea.[33]

The charge scale is both inflated and deflated by the tension between the real and the legal offense. The lesser offense is assumed to be masking a greater offense, inviting suspicions and inquiries to pierce the formal record. At the same time, the charging scale is forced downward in a plain frustration of legislative purpose. If minor burglaries are treated as larcenies, what about minor larcenies? If lesser assaults are viewed as breaches of the peace or disorderly conduct, what is left of a criminal code that has been drafted with rational gradations of culpability and sanction? As the minor charge classes are "filled" with initially more serious but discounted offenses, it becomes difficult for the prosecutor or anyone else to take a minor charge at face value. At some point, such petty offenses may not seem worthy of prosecution at all, and the more serious offenses are distorted beyond recognition.

It is time for the courts to assert an independent interest in the accuracy of pleas, entirely apart from the preferences of the parties. As Newman suggests, "the more specific objective of accuracy of the plea" should be treated on its own terms, separated from the question of voluntariness.[34] Otherwise, the nature and meaning of a statutory body of criminal law is left to partisans inevitably captive of their role—

a prosecutor involved in the "competitive enterprise of ferreting out crime" and a defendant understandably concerned with minimizing harm to himself. The judge should reject a plea that concedes facts which are erroneous or omits facts in order to make the offense appear less serious. And he should not accept a plea to a lesser offense if the facts plainly support a greater charge. His rejection will in the ordinary course result in prosecution of the greater charge, even if he cannot compel it. There are, of course, borderline issues where statutory definitions have been deliberately written by the legislature to permit prosecutors to take correctional factors into account—as in the mental states associated with the degrees of homicide. These judgments should be made by the prosecutor. But the accuracy issue should not be confused with issues of sentencing that are best left to a judge who can exercise *his* discretion to take into account the defendant's contrition, cooperation with the authorities, or rehabilitative potential.

For most cases, there is no need to vest the parties with the power to distort the charge. The judge can suspend sentence, impose probation, or approve dismissal of the charge, thereby permitting most of the objectives sought by the prosecutor to be achieved. It is only when the legislature has denied to courts the authority to sentence below certain limits that the same sentencing outcome may not be obtained from the judge as from the prosecutor's reduction of the charge. Yet it is in just such cases that the use of inaccurate pleas most clearly violates the legislative purpose to restrict sentencing discretion. If a principle of necessary discretion must be created for these exceptional cases, on either constitutional or practical grounds, it should be a limited one—operative only when the prosecutor can persuade the judge that an accurate plea must be sacrificed in order to achieve overriding objectives of the criminal law—such as cooperation in law enforcement or a required minimum of individualization or rationality.[35]

C. The Judge's Discretion

Even if the plea is plainly voluntary and is made to a charge that has a "factual basis," the judge may reject it in the exercise of a "sound judicial discretion."[36] In doing so, he is obligated to consider the prosecutor's views, but he is not bound by them. As the American Bar Association *Standards* remind us, the trial judge "should reach an independent decision on whether to grant charge or sentence concessions" and should approve them only "when the interest of the public in the effective administration of criminal justice would thereby be served."[37] *Frady* v. *People* illustrates when rejection may be in order. Frady "had been of service to the state" in obtaining the conviction of his codefendant on the greater charge of murder in the first degree. Nevertheless, the court concluded that the trial judge did not abuse his discretion when he rejected Frady's plea to second-degree murder, endorsed by the prosecutor, because the two defendants were comparably culpable.[38] The judge's freedom to reject the prosecutor's recommendation, however, does not extend to accepting a guilty plea to a lesser charge without the prosecutor's consent. In *State* v. *Carlson*, a trial judge was held to have exceeded his authority when he tried to accept, over the prosecutor's objection, a murder defendant's plea of guilty to manslaughter. "[A]lthough the court may judicially determine the disposition of a charge based on the evidence, the law and its sentencing power, it may not, in effect, usurp the executive function of choosing which charge to initiate based on defendant's willingness to plead guilty to a lesser offense. . . . Here the trial judge, with the defendant's agreement, was in effect ordering the district attorney not to prosecute the murder charge against Vail."[39]

A group of Michigan cases develops the distinction between the executive and the judicial power more fully. They describe as an "executive function" the prosecutor's duty to determine under which of two applicable statutes a prosecution will be instituted. "For the judiciary to claim power to control the institution and conduct of prosecutions would be . . . a violation of the constitutional separation of powers."[40] A trial judge was reversed for directing a prosecutor to proceed on a higher charge that he had wanted to drop for lack of evidence.[41] In *People* v. *Matulonis*, the trial judge was asked by the prosecutor to substitute a count of attempted felonious assault, carrying a maximum sentence of two years, for a charge of assault with intent to commit great bodily harm, which provided an eight-year maximum sentence, and to accept the defendant's plea to the lesser charge. The police officer and the victim opposed the agreement. The judge rejected the plea and the defendant was convicted of the original charge. On appeal, the defendant urged that the judge had exercised so much control over the prosecution that he had violated the separation of powers. The court of appeals agreed, holding that the trial judge had "failed to reserve" his authority to reject a plea "to the kind of extreme cases in which it is warranted."[42]

The most complete discussion of the authority of the judge to reject a plea bargain recommended by the prosecutor is to be found in *United States* v. *Ammidown*. Ammidown had been charged with first-degree murder for serving as a "hired gun" for a husband in a conspiracy to kill his wife. His plea to murder in the second degree was rejected by the judge because "his crime was so heinous and the evidence of guilt so overwhelming" that the public interest required trial on the greater charge.[43] Ammidown was subsequently convicted of murder in the first degree. On appeal, Judge Harold Leventhal treated the charging power as intrinsically executive but as inevitably impinging on matters that are intrinsically judicial.

Canvassing the cases on judicial review of dismissals, Leventhal concluded that a judge must have greater authority in the case of a "diluted dismissal"—"when the case is not entirely dismissed as to a defendant but he has received a substantial sentence for a phase of the same offense." The court must be able "to forestall gross abuses of prosecutorial discretion." Among the abuses he noted is permitting "the plea bargain to become the means whereby the hardened criminal escapes justice."[44] Several guidelines were provided for the trial judge's "reasoned exercise of . . . discretion." First, the prosecutor's recommendation should be followed in the "overwhelming number of cases," because he can best evaluate the relation between "the government's prosecution resources and the number of cases it is able to prosecute." Second, the judge should be more than a "rubber stamp" and must see to it that the public interest is protected. Third, a plea agreement should be rejected only when necessary in order to be fair to the defendant or prosecution or to protect the court's sentencing authority. He gave no hint when fairness to the defendant might lead a court to reject a plea that the defendant preferred, in the belief it was in his best interest. As to the prosecutorial interest, the court could reject a plea favored by the prosecutor if he had abused his discretion by failing to consider "factors that must be given consideration in the public interest, factors such as the deterrent aspects of the criminal law." But it would have to be a "blatant and extreme case"—a standard similar to *Cowan*'s requirement that discretion "should not be disturbed unless clearly contrary to manifest public interest."[45] If the bargain was intended to achieve a legitimate prosecutorial purpose, as where there existed "an insufficiency of evidence, a doubt as to the admissibility of certain evidence under exclusionary rules, a need for evidence to bring another felon to justice, or other similar consideration," a diminution in the judge's sentencing discretion would have to be tolerated.

Applying these criteria in *Ammidown*, the court concluded that the trial judge had no grounds for rejecting the plea. There was no claim of unfairness to the defendant. The prosecutor had adequately considered the public interest. He had told the court the bargain would both assure the successful prosecution of an accomplice (the husband) and "neutralize" the defendant (the "hired gun") by convicting him on a lesser but quite substantial charge. And the differences between the sentences available on the two charges were insufficient to warrant rejection of the plea. "Where vigorous prosecution of one case threatens to undermine successful prosecution of another, it has traditionally been the prosecutor who determines which case will be pressed to conclusion, and his decision has been given great deference by the courts."[46] The case was remanded with instructions to accept the plea of guilty to second degree murder.

The United States Court of Appeals for the Fifth Circuit has accepted *Ammidown*'s general teaching that "the district court's role . . . [is] secondary and complementary to that of the prosecutor."[47] The district court may not, for example, bar "plea agreements of the kind where the prosecution drops some charges in exchange for the defendant's plea to other charges." But the court balked at adopting "abuse of discretion" as the standard for rejecting a plea bargain recommended by the prosecutor. It refused "to accept without question the prosecutor's view of the public good" and rejected a plea that would "result in the defendant's receiving too light a sentence."[48]

Despite the occasional differences in emphasis, the structure for reviewing prosecutorial discretion is clearly established in the judge's authority not only over guilty pleas but over dismissals and charge reductions. And viable standards for review exist as well. "While there obviously is a separation of powers issue lurking in the background, it can hardly be doubted that the judiciary has inherent power to control abuse or misuse of prosecutorial power. . . . It is one thing to assert that prosecutorial discretion in declining to initiate a prosecution is unreviewable. It is quite another to say that once an indictment has been filed and the trial court has obtained jurisdiction of the case, it has no power to control prosecutorial overreaching, particularly when such overreaching adversely affects expedition of the calendar and other significant aspects of judicial administration, not to mention the all-important matter of proper correctional disposition of the defendant."[49] Nevertheless, courts have been curiously passive in using the structure or the standards, feeling themselves constrained by unarticulated notions of institutional incompetence and by the ghosts of history. In the next chapter, I shall show that the separation of powers argument is overstated; that it rests on a misunderstanding of the concept of discretion; and that it should not inhibit the development of a common law of prosecutorial discretion.

III.

A COMMON LAW OF PROSECUTORIAL DISCRETION

The dominant reform approach to the problem of prosecutorial discretion in recent years has been the establishment of standards and guidelines by the county prosecutor himself or by the agency of which he is a subordinate. The most elaborate of these are the *Principles of Prosecution* recently issued by the United States Department of Justice.[1] Virtually no one, however, has considered how such guidelines would fare in the courts or whether it would be preferable to follow a more traditional course of common-law development, with rules emerging case by case until they have passed an experimental period and are genuinely ripe for legislation—whether through statutes or agency regulations. It has been assumed, without much discussion, that the courts are not competent to deal with such questions or that they are already too busy or that they would compromise their neutrality if they were to review the prosecutor's decisions with care. On the rare occasions when these matters have been pressed, the doctrine of separation of powers has been advanced as the basic reason for restricting the role of the courts.

A. The Problem of Separation of Powers

The separation-of-powers doctrine asserts that certain functions may be exercised only by a particular branch of government, that such functions cannot be delegated to any other branch, and that one department may not interfere with another by usurping its powers or by supervising their exercise. At the same time, it recognizes that separation cannot be absolute. Madison, among others, conceded that the blending of powers in each branch might be necessary if each was to defend its position in the constitutional system. The pardon power of the executive and the impeachment power of Congress, both judicial in nature, illustrate that point in the Constitution. And the dramatic development of administrative law, with its blending of legislative, executive, and judicial powers, has confirmed it. The doctrine is in essence a statement of competing themes, cautioning against commingling of powers while accepting the need for blending them. It places few real limits on judicial review, and fewer on the states than on the federal government.[2]

The emerging law of dismissals, guilty pleas, and discriminatory prosecution presents no real threat to the separation of powers. Each of the standards of review used—"rationality," "abuse of discretion," "clearly contrary to manifest public interest," and "bad faith"—turns on the principle that a prosecutor's decision may be reversed only when it undermines the authority constitutionally assigned to the judiciary. *Ammidown* relied on that principle when it noted that a prosecutor cannot use dismissals to usurp the judge's sentencing authority.[3] And *Cowan* concluded that the courts must perform the "essential judicial function" of "protecting the public interest in the evenhanded administration of criminal justice."[4] The distinction between "judicial usurpation of discretionary authority and review of the statutory and constitutional limits to that authority" is one that "the law has long recognized"[5] in dealing with executive discretion generally, and prosecutorial discretion is no different.

The absolutist position, which denies any reviewing role to the courts, persists only in cases involving initiation of prosecution,[6] but even there the position traces less to the Constitution than to a common-law doctrine of *nolle prosequi* based upon the authority enjoyed by the English attorney general in a system of private prosecution. Federal and state constitutions make no explicit grant of prosecutorial discretion. It is doubtful, for example, that the doctrine of separation of powers alone would prohibit Congress from eliminating such discretion if it chose to do so—*e.g.*, by enacting statutes that mandate investigation or prosecution upon a particular showing and that enforce the statutory criteria by judicial review or by private litigation. As the court noted in *Powell* v. *Katzenbach*, "we will assume, without deciding, that where Congress has withdrawn all discretion from the prosecutor by special legislation, a court might be empowered to force prosecutions in some circumstances."[7] Many states provide explicitly for a judicial role in prosecution, even including judicial appointment of prosecutors and judicial direction to initiate a prosecution.[8]

Judicial resistance to supervision of prosecutorial discretion at any of its several stages probably stems more from concern about the difficulties of the task than from constitutional doctrine. This is evident in the effect of separation-of-powers considerations on the outcome of cases. All the leading appellate opinions reverse the trial judge when he refuses to accept the prosecutor's decision. While upholding the idea of judicial review, they apply a standard that makes it doubtful that anything but an egregious decision by the prosecutor could properly be disregarded. Their actions reflect a belief that they are unable, as a practical and a legal matter, to compel the prosecutor to abide by their decision. "Few subjects" said Chief Justice Warren Burger, then a circuit judge, "are less adapted to judicial review than the exercise by the Executive of his discretion" in these matters.[9] The point has been repeated often and has led reformers to minimize the judicial role and to look instead to legislation or to prosecutorially established guidelines.

Yet the prosecutor's decisions are no more intricate than others routinely dealt with by judges. They are probably less so because they are made in contexts with which judges are familiar and involve questions that are integral to the judge's function—weight and sufficiency of evidence, correctional considerations, statutory interpretation, and constitutional law. In cases that begin with an arrest, it is the police who gather the facts and make the principal judgments on investigative methods and enforcement priorities; the prosecutor's role is almost judicial in nature and consists of screening witness statements and assessing their sufficiency. There is nothing inherently executive in the skills he uses in weighing credibility and appraising the weight of evidence. There is even less that is inherently executive in deciding which statute has been violated or whether correctional considerations are relevant. Even when a prosecutor uses an investigative grand jury, a distinction must be made between his role in leading an investigation and in appraising its product as a basis for indictment. Only when the investigative role is dominant —when he is allocating resources, emphasizing one strategy of enforcement rather than another, choosing a particular method of investigation—can the prosecutor be said to have special competence and to deserve unusual deference. Otherwise, he is merely the first law-trained official to determine whether there is enough evidence to warrant a charge, but one who is deprived by his role of the judicial attributes of neutrality and impartiality.

The fear that there is no realistic way for courts to "compel a prosecutor to proceed if he does not wish to do so" is an exaggerated one. Consider, for example, the reasons offered by Charles Wright. He says the prosecutor can easily defeat the court's effort to review dismissals by indicating "to the jury . . . in his opening statement . . . and in his presentation of evidence . . . the considerations that should work an acquittal." The same point is made in the Comments to the new *Uniform Rules of Criminal Procedure.*[10] These assertions confuse the prosecutor's power to ignore the law (and get away with it) with what he may lawfully do—just as some confuse the jury's power to disregard the law it is sworn to apply with its authority to do so. The courts have consistently rejected the idea that the jury's power to nullify law should be converted into a right. Similarly, a prosecutor does not have complete latitude "in his opening statement." A body of law circumscribes what he may say. There is no reason to assume prosecutors will ignore either that body of law or their legal obligations with regard to "presentation of evidence." If prosecutors act contrary to their legal or ethical obligations, the court can order a mistrial, or it can tell the jury to disregard what the prosecutor has said, or it can expose him to the risk of disciplinary proceedings. The prosecutor may, of course, try to avoid judicial direction by acting in less visible ways. But the judge, too, has effective power. If the prosecutor will not accept judicial control of dismissals, the judge may find it necessary to exercise his discretion to reject plea bargains, motions to dismiss, or recommendations regarding sentence.

Wright's position—and at bottom Judge Weinfeld's in *Greater Blouse*—treats the confrontation case as identical with the routine one. This is a mistake. Just as judges are not champing at the bit to appoint special prosecutors, so too are prosecutors not prepared routinely to do battle with judges. There is every reason to assume that the judge's order will be obeyed. His denial of a motion to dismiss or his rejection of a guilty plea will ordinarily be followed by nothing more serious than the prosecutor's telling the defendant that an arrangement cannot be made, allowing him to withdraw his guilty plea, and proceeding to trial.[11] And a system of appellate review assures that trial judges will not assert their power arbitrarily. If at the end of that process, there is still a confrontation between the courts and the district attorney, the appointment of a special prosecutor may be an option of last resort.

The explanation for judicial passivity plainly runs deeper than the fear of being overwhelmed by the pressures of the docket, or feelings of incompetence or inability to obtain compliance. It is rooted in a misunderstanding of the relation between the concept of discretion itself and the separation of powers. The absence of a clear-cut legal rule defined by the legislature is treated by the courts as if it endows the prosecutor not only with discretion to fill the interstices in the rule but with an exclusively "executive" authority to do so. Discretion, in this view, is essentially "lawless" and exists "whenever the effective limits on [an official's] power leave him free to make a choice among possible courses of action or inaction."[12] Professors Mortimer and Sanford Kadish use the concept of "legitimated interposition" to describe how judicial acquiescence in the prosecutor's "rule departures" converts them over time into the "justifiable exercise of an explicitly delegated discretion."[13]

The exercise of discretion is neither lawless nor a prerogative of the executive branch. All officials, whether in the executive or the judical branch, must make reasoned judgments within the scope of an authority often left deliberately vague by the legislature. They are obligated to act in accordance with legal principles—in some instances taking a primary and initiating role, in others taking a secondary and reactive one[14]—sharing a process for filling the interstices of statutes and competing policies. In the end, however, it is the courts that have the ultimate authority to distinguish between the administrative matters that should be left to the prosecutor and the legal rules and policies whose development judges should share with him.

B. Building a Common Law: Some Illustrations

A substantial body of research as well as the guidelines recently issued tells us why the prosecutor asks the court to dismiss or reduce a charge or to accept a guilty plea. His request may be based on evidentiary grounds or on the desire to facilitate another prosecution by obtaining the defendant's cooperation. He may wish to lighten an overly heavy case load or obtain treatment for a defendant in a noncriminal process. He may be following a policy of nonenforcement of certain crimes or trying to gain some procedural advantage, or he may want to avoid the risk of trial.

In this section, I shall consider how judges might deal with such reasons, case by case, in order to illustrate the rules and distinctions that may be fashioned in building a common law of prosecutorial discretion—whether that discretion is exercised pursuant to guidelines or on an *ad hoc* basis.

The decision on sufficiency of evidence is least controversial. It does not really involve discretion as such, but rather an appraisal of the credibility of witnesses and an assessment of the weight of the evidence in light of legal requirements. If the facts are not in dispute, the prosecutor is obligated to charge unless he can justify a decision not to do so on some other ground. He has no discretion to ignore or to nullify the criminal law. It is when the facts are disputed that evidentiary judgments are sometimes incorrectly characterized as discretionary in nature. Properly viewed, however, he has a duty to make such judgments in order to get the process moving, even as a judge and jury will have to do at later stages. They may be difficult but they are part of his legal obligation to charge crime. There is little dispute that when dismissal or charge reduction is based on evidentiary grounds, the prosecutor's decision should be deferred to, but the deference is not without limit. For example, the prosecutor may not characterize credible and sufficient testimony as incredible and insufficient. When he does so, he is not exercising a discretion allowed him by law. If he uses evidentiary labels to provide an acceptable patina for conclusions reached on other grounds, if he uses ambiguous statutory language to conceal overcharging, if he offers the dismissal of charges not supported by the evidence, he is abusing his authority. If defendants against whom the case is weak routinely obtain more substantial charge and sentence concessions than plainly guilty ones, because the prosecutor fears an adverse verdict in the former case, he may be engaging in disparate treatment that cannot be justified on rational grounds and may also be impinging on the judge's sentencing authority.

The prosecutor must often choose among several statutes applicable to the same set of facts, *e.g.*, assault with a dangerous weapon and assault with intent to kill, or he must choose among several degrees of crime, whether the charge should be murder or manslaughter, rape or indecent assault, robbery or larceny. Where these choices depend on facts that are uncertain, they deserve the same deference as his decisions on evidentiary matters. But where the facts are undisputed and the choices are made on policy grounds, the situation is more complicated. If the facts plainly show rape, for example, and the prosecutor is not busy, it is not clear why a plea to the lesser offense of indecent assault should not be rejected—as contrary to the manifest public interest in enforcing criminal law—unless the prosecutor can furnish a rational basis for accepting it. Such a basis may perhaps be found in the defendant's cooperation in providing information, in minimizing the cost of trial, in the fact that defendant is a first offender, or in the prosecutor's workload. Even then, however, such factors should be submitted to the judge, who may take them into account when he decides whether to approve dismissal or charge reduction. Or they should be taken into account by the judge when he makes his sentencing determination with the aid of his probation officer. They should not be used by the prosecutor to distort the initial charge.

May prosecutors rely on correctional factors as a basis for choosing or retaining a charge, or fixing on the number of charges? May the prosecutor, for example, follow a practice of dismissing charges against auto thieves who are teenagers and first offenders? May he routinely dismiss minor embezzlement cases when the defendant has made restitution? May he "divert" the offender towards psychiatric treatment or to assistance from social agencies? May he rely on such grounds to charge a lesser offense or fewer than all the offenses committed—to charge indecent assault rather than rape, larceny rather than robbery, one forgery count rather than twelve? Since the charge provides the upper limit for the sentence, such practices raise squarely the question whether the prosecutor is intruding on the judge's sentencing powers, particularly since his actions are often based on rehabilitative or compassionate grounds.

A good deal may be said, of course, for avoiding conviction whenever possible and for minimizing the stigma associated with the criminal sanction. But there are considerations of the deepest moment pointing in the other direction. Dismissals and charge reductions may reduce the exemplary power of the all-too-rare conviction. They may frustrate the effort to make sentencing more rational by relying on probation officers and presentence reports.[15] And they may mislead the defendant by not producing the lighter sentence that induced his plea, because the sentence is often based on the "real" offense rather than the adjudicated one. A study in the District of Columbia, for example, noted that "contrary to expectation, sentencing concessions were not awarded routinely to defendants who entered guilty pleas. In fact, no concessions were apparent for assault and larceny cases. For burglary, many guilty pleas followed charge reductions, but there was no evidence that these charge reductions resulted in lenient sentences. Only for the robbery offenses were sentences more severe for offenders convicted at trial."[16] A court confronting these questions might conclude that the prosecutor's reliance on correctional factors is an entirely rational accommodation of competing policies. It might as easily conclude, however, that such use of the charging and dismissal power intrudes on the judicial function, that it often misleads defendants, and that the prosecutor should content himself with making appropriate recommendations to sentencing judges and pardoning authorities.

Should courts inquire into dismissals and guilty pleas to ascertain if they reflect a policy of unequal treatment or discriminatory prosecution? Under existing law, a defendant may have the case against him dismissed if he is prosecuted when other similarly situated persons have not been—if he can show that the prosecution is "deliberately based upon an unjustifiable standard such as race, religion, or other arbitrary classification." But the issue of equal treatment need not be confined to the constitutional minimum. In exercising his responsibility to assure that dismissals and guilty pleas are consistent with the effective administration of justice, it would be entirely proper for a judge to inquire routinely as to whether similar defendants have been afforded the same opportunities as the defendant.[17] Where dismissal is sought, the prosecutor might be required to explain his reasons for not going forward in a class of case that is regularly prosecuted; where a plea agreement is involved, an explanation might be required for insisting on conviction of a crime usually dismissed or not charged at all. If such inquiry were regularly made by the courts, the larger issues of policy governing the prosecutor's actions would quickly emerge. For example: Should courts be satisfied with a prosecutor's policy of singling out one member of a class of similarly situated income tax evaders because he feels that only one highly visible prosecution is needed to achieve the objective of general deterrence? May he devote greater resources to investigating and prosecuting one segment of an industry rather than another, one profession rather than another? May he routinely abandon prosecution of minor assaults by one spouse on another, one black on another, or in inner city high crime areas? Are crimes among strangers to be more vigorously prosecuted than those among persons with prior relationships? By insisting on a rationale for law enforcement in the interests of equal application of the law, the courts would force articulation by the prosecutor of how his strategies relate to the objectives of the criminal law. Most of these strategies would be upheld because they are rational accommodations of overlapping or conflicting statutes and available resources. But the process of challenge and justification would over time provide a basis for assessing the relative competences of judge and prosecutor—not in an all-or-nothing pattern of deference or intervention but in relation to particular subjects in particular factual settings.

The premise underlying a rule requiring justification for disparate treatment, even when it does not violate the equal protection clause, is the principle articulated in *State v. Winne* and in the desuetude cases. A prosecutor may not decide to abandon the enforcement of a criminal statute. He may not nullify the criminal law. In doing so, he intrudes on the legislature's law-making authority, the judge's sentencing authority, and the interest of the victims whose surrogate he is. Moreover, he may deprive victims of restitutionary rights they may otherwise have if the charges are brought and adjudicated. When full enforcement is not possible—because resources are scarce or because statutes and policies conflict—a policy of nonenforcement that is both selective and rational is preferable. For example, a distinction might be made between cases plainly affected with a public interest and those which seem private and domestic, enforcing the former more often and more visibly than the latter, particularly if noncriminal alternatives such as restitution or peace bonds are available. When resources are ample, however, a policy of total nonenforcement should not be condoned, even if there are difficulties in learning of the policy or framing a remedy for it. Indeed, as will be suggested later, it may be desirable to define a role for the victim to assist the court in dealing with the problem.

When a charge is adequately based in law and fact, may the prosecutor use it to induce a defendant or a potential defendant to become a government witness, promising him complete immunity from prosecution or a reduction in the number and gravity of the charges? At present, there is no way for the judge to deal with such informal immunity beforehand, so that he may pass on the propriety of the arrangement. As a result, the opinion in *Santobello* virtually dictates that a prosecutor's promise of immunity must be treated as a *fait accompli*. If instead the prosecutor were required first to file the charge and then to move to dismiss it on "cooperation" grounds, the hearing on the motion would provide the judge with an opportunity to consider the matter. He could then decide whether the statutory immunity procedure must be followed, or he could assess the propriety of the arrangement on its merits. Without such a hearing, there is a genuine risk that the prosecutor may be intruding on the judge's sentencing powers, endorsing unequal treatment, or subverting the judge's authority over guilty pleas. Judicial review in such cases should, of course, be limited, because judges are rarely in a position to weigh the relative importance of two prosecutions or the effect of one upon the other. But unless the facts are before him, the judge cannot determine whether the grant of immunity conforms to a rational policy that is being rationally administered.

How should courts deal with dismissals or charge reductions sought by the prosecutor on tactical grounds, or in order to reduce his workload or the court's? When a prosecutor seeks tactical advantage, he is more an advocate than an official serving the public interest and should not be protected from close judicial scrutiny. The workload issue is more complicated. Court congestion would seem to be the court's business, not the prosecutor's. And the California courts have held it is an abuse of judicial discretion for a trial judge to dismiss a case in order to reduce the pressure of cases.[18] Is it also an abuse of discretion for the prosecutor to dismiss or reduce charges on grounds that his office is overworked? Probably not. If the pressure of business is genuine, not asserted as a cover for more substantive grounds, the prosecutor must be allowed to regulate the flow of cases. He is especially competent to assess his case load and the probable cost in prosecutorial resources. But the existence of an overburdened office should not be the only ground for dismissal or reduction. It is too mechanical a factor to stand alone. At most, it should be used to enhance the plausibility of other more substantive grounds for decision.

The prosecutor's decision on charge reductions and on other aspects of charging, dismissals, and guilty pleas may turn on fact questions, resource questions, or questions of investigative feasibility and priority. These matters must be left primarily to the prosecutor. But his decisions may also raise questions that are legal in nature and plainly within the judge's competence and obligation, such as statutory interpretation and sentencing policy, the extent to which enforcement may be abandoned or may be conducted selectively, the degree to which police illegality may be masked by agreements on reduced or fewer charges, and the relation between one or more of these and the larger objectives of the criminal law—retributive, deterrent, and correctional. The judge can know which of these is involved only if he elicits from the prosecutor his reasons for seeking a dismissal, charge reduction, or guilty plea. He may learn that the prosecutor is serving the interests of his docket, treating some laws as less important than others, making strategic judgments as to which offense should be prosecuted and how often, prosecuting crimes among strangers more energetically than those involving a prior relationship. Each of these grounds may be a rational basis for his actions. But unless they are brought into the open, each justification lined up with its decision, the judge has no way to exercise the "sound judicial discretion" demanded of him.

The implications of such measures for the guilty plea are fairly clear. Where facts and law are not contested, convictions—whether by guilty plea or trial—should be "on the nose," leaving correctional considerations to the sentence, not the charge. If the legislature has not individualized justice enough, as in the scheme of fixed sentences, or if it has individualized too much, as in a scheme of broadly indeterminate sentences, the remedy should not be in the prosecutor's hands alone. Rejection of legislative commands should lie with the courts, in appropriately limited circumstances, or with the people. Efforts to reconcile conflicting legislative purposes and to accommodate enforcement considerations should be for the prosecutor in the first instance, but always in a manner accountable to the courts. If cooperation is to be rewarded, it should be done by the judge in the course of sentencing, not through manipulation of the charge. And if that prospect is not enough to induce cooperation, the prosecutor should be required to seek formal immunity for the person whose cooperation he seeks.

Where facts and law are contested, there should be plea discussions but not plea bargains.[19] Such discussions may demonstrate that the prosecutor is not confident that he can establish guilt in the degree charged, in which event he should reduce the charge, not use it as a lever to force concessions from the defendant. It may emerge that he has charged more offenses than he can establish, in which event the excess should be dismissed. By exchanging information and interpretations of facts and law, the parties' assessments of the probability of conviction or acquittal may change and they may reach agreement on a guilty plea that accurately reflects uncontested facts, particularly if individualizing factors will be considered only at sentencing.

There is no real danger that judicial review of guilty pleas will bring an end to such pleas. Most defendants plead guilty because they have no defenses and, above all, because they will gain a sentencing advantage by cooperation. What judicial review will do is shift control of the system's norms from the prosecutor to the judge and begin the development of a textured common law of prosecutorial authority. And that will force the prosecutor to be more attentive to legislative commands and to feel a greater obligation to develop rational enforcement policies.[20]

C. A More Active Role for the Judge

Judicial review of dismissals, guilty pleas, and immunity grants is uniquely suited for the development of standards that would reconcile the prosecutor's discretion with the public interest in accuracy and legality. No such development will occur, however, if it is left to the parties—prosecution and defense—to bring the relevant considerations before the courts. Instead, a new set of ritualized phrases will emerge that, on their face, will state a rational basis. A significant change will take place only if judges take more initiatives. It need not follow that they would then be transformed into law enforcement officers. The prosecutor would continue to be the official primarily obligated to determine what offense to charge. But he would no longer be permitted to conceal policy judgments behind evidentiary rubrics. The judge would determine whether dismissals and guilty pleas are based on accurate facts, whether they are the result of improper pressures and inducements, whether they reflect rational enforcement policies and reasonable interpretations of competing statutory and constitutional provisions, whether the sentences recommended are sensibly related to the underlying facts and charges.

We have seen, however, that judicial review of the prosecutor has foundered in the past because it has met strong institutional resistance from prosecutors positioned to take initiatives and from judges conditioned to be acquiescent.[21] Effective supervision of the prosecutor may turn, therefore, on developing procedures that will take judges beyond the assertions of the parties. Several devices come to mind. The judge may begin by placing a burden on the parties, especially the prosecutor, to justify dismissals and guilty pleas and the arrangements surrounding them. He can also make better use of the prosecutor's file to assist him in the search for a rational basis for the plea, a "sound basis" for the exercise of judicial discretion, or a verification of the prosecutor's assertions as to the facts. At a minimum, the file should contain material that would enable a reviewing judge to test assertions that originally credible witnesses have become incredible or are no longer available or to ascertain that there is substantial evidence of the major charge and thereby assure that the prosecutor was not "overcharging" and using bluff to induce a guilty plea, that the correctional considerations asserted for reducing a charge are valid, and that immunity arrangements have been approved. The judge may have to call witnesses on occasion, not only for verification purposes but to make it plain that he will not always rely on the file alone. Even then, he may need the assistance of a genuine adversary such as the victim—in the administrative settings as distinct from the trial—to challenge the consensus all too likely to be presented to him by prosecution and defense.

In discussing the need for a greater judicial role, it is sometimes suggested that a distinction should be made between the majority of states, where prosecution is a county matter, and the federal system and those few states where it is organized more centrally and hierarchically. The suggestion turns on the point that a hierarchical system headed by a cabinet member genuinely deserves the deference accorded the executive branch under the principle of separation of powers. It is large enough and politically responsible enough to establish rules and internal review procedures that transcend the local prosecutor. An analogy exists in the two different roles defined for the courts under the Model Immunity Act—the first, for states where there is an attorney general and no significant judicial review, and the second, for those where criminal law is enforced on a county basis and judges are expected to play a part in reviewing immunity grants "in the public interest." The point is valid, but it will have only limited utility until a common law of prosecutorial discretion provides a basis for defining the relation between judge and prosecutor more closely. Even then, its utility lies principally in suggesting the degree of deference to be paid by judges to carefully formulated rules of general applicability, particularly if they emerge from rulemaking proceedings that are legislative in nature.[22] It does not eliminate the question whether some of the principles, however equally applied, intrude upon legislative and judicial prerogatives. As to these, the courts must remain the ultimate authority.

D. A Role for the Victim

The prosecutor is pressed by his role and function and by his sense of priorities—political, legal, and administrative—to modify the criminal law. His modifications may be the fine tuning we need to adjust a complex legal system; or they may be done *ad hoc* and reflect very little reasoned consideration. How can we assure ourselves that the prosecutor's decisions on charging, dismissals, and guilty pleas will take into account the full range of relevant interests? We usually think of defense counsel, and the adversary process, as providing the necessary counterweight to the prosecutor. A dialectic is said to be at work, with thesis and antithesis as to law and fact presented at every stage and culminating in a synthesis carefully honed by the judge. That, however, is the rhythm and the rhetoric of a contested trial. Decisions on charges and guilty pleas are very different. The usual check on official power provided by an adversary system is simply not operative in these administrative and consensual settings. By the time the matter is presented to a court, defense counsel and prosecutor may no longer be at odds; they may be in agreement and have a stake in blurring the underlying facts. In theory, the judge is relied on to provide the necessary corrections. But we have seen that the judge—so "imperial" elsewhere in his assertion of judicial control over executive power—is curiously passive in relation to the prosecutor's discretion and to the plea arrangements made by prosecutor and defense counsel.

A partial solution might lie in giving the victim a greater stake in the prosecution—not occasionally, intermittently, and by sufferance, but routinely, as of right, at set stages in the course of a criminal proceeding.[23] Prosecutor and judge might then be made more accountable, and public confidence in the rule of law would be increased. Undoubtedly, there are problems in taking such an approach. The criminal justice system is already so burdened that it may not be able to stand any change that might require more time and more money. And victims may be too vindictive, wanting full enforcement, more charges, and heavier sentences when less-than-full enforcement would better serve the public interest.

There is evidence, however, that the risk of added vindictiveness is overstated. Victims are even more varied than the crimes committed against them. In the vast number of regulatory offenses, the "victim" is often the public agency vested with primary responsibility for protecting a segment of the public interest. In the more conventional cases, the criminal charge is little more than a point of entry for troubled people seeking solutions to a remarkable range of problems. Their claims are often civil in nature and come to the criminal process only because the victim thinks a show of public force is necessary to get relief. For example, in cases of minor theft, bad checks, fraud, or property damage, the victim has little or no interest in imprisonment or in pressing the criminal charge; he wants monetary compensation or restitution. In cases of domestic violence and neighborhood disputes, the criminal complaint is often a call for official help in deteriorating relationships, not for criminal prosecution. Giving victims a stake in the criminal process in such cases is a way of reducing, not adding to, the quantum of retributive impulses by directing them to processes of mediation and conciliation, sometimes augmented by financial settlements and some species of injunctive relief.[24]

An entirely different set of problems is presented by crimes of violence unmitigated by prior relationship, serious invasions of property, thefts above the nuisance level, and corruption. Such crimes comprise too important a part of the public sense of justice to be enforced or not as a victim chooses. They suffer today from too little enforcement, often because the victim is unwilling to cooperate in a prosecution that no longer seems to have much relation to him. What started out as *his* injury has been so entirely taken over by police or prosecutor that the victim no longer feels a proprietary interest in seeing it through to completion. There is little hope of reawakening that interest if we continue treating the victim as incidental to the process—rarely consulting him, rarely even telling him whether the crime he reported was prosecuted or whether the charge was dismissed, reduced, or bargained out. If we are to maintain the credibility of the criminal sanction, we must persuade such victims to again play their role, even if they are moved to do so by vindictive feelings.

We should expand on recent experiments with putting victims back into the system—not only by prosecutors consulting them after arrest or probation officers interviewing them before sentencing—but by authorizing them formally to participate in decisions on dismissals, charge reductions, guilty pleas, and sentencing.[25] They would provide an initiative that is desperately needed if we are to have any hope of judges supervising these stages of the criminal process. The fact is that judges are accustomed to relying on the initiative of others, and such initiatives do not exist when prosecutor and defense counsel have settled matters between them. Placing the victim in the process would force the prosecutor to justify to the court his decision not to proceed, or to proceed on assumptions about the facts and the law which differ from the victim's account. It would provide the judge with a party who has a genuine interest in challenging and correcting the version of fact and law proffered by the prosecutor or defense counsel or both. What is now judicial acquiescence in an administrative decision or a consensual process would be converted to an occasion when the judge would expect an accounting. The prosecutor would have to identify for the court why the public interest is different from the victim's. The judge would have to determine whether the prosecutor has a rational basis for his actions—one consistent with statutory and constitutional requirements. And the system would have the benefit of a jurisprudence of competing interests, presented by persons who have a genuine stake in them.

We cannot eliminate the judgments that must be made in charging crime or in dismissing or reducing charges. But, as Kenneth Davis urges, we can confine, structure, and check them.[26] The error of most recent commentators is in accepting the shibboleth that the judge cannot play an effective role in the process. By putting aside the possibilities afforded by genuine judicial review of motions to dismiss, reduce charges, or accept guilty pleas, the courts have too long ignored not only the history of the common law in building standards case by case but also the more recent body of administrative law in which courts have balanced legality with the need to defer to special competence.

The most important consequence of judicial review—if it is reinforced by occasional denial of motions to dismiss or rejection of guilty pleas—is that it would make the prosecutor more accountable. He would have to explain and justify his departures from the formal rules, and his explanations would become subject to verification. In some offices, sensible policies, rationally administered, would be exposed to view and the judicial role would be minimal. In other offices, where policies are not consistent, a burden of justification would reduce disparate treatment or require a rational basis for it. And it would minimize the use of bogus rationalizations to mask the real decision rules. Case-by-case articulation of the grounds for decision will bring to the fore competing statutory policies and the need for closer definition of what is best left to the executive branch and what is to be decided by the judiciary.

There is, of course, a genuine risk that judges may intrude too much, assuming "executive" functions, adding to burdens already too heavy in many jurisdictions, and compromising their neutrality and impartiality. To guard against the risk, the prosecutor should retain absolute authority to initiate prosecution, though the total insulation of that decision may change as judges at later stages become more familiar with the charging process. It can be expected not only that the prosecutors will be affected by how judges deal with charges at subsequent stages of the process, even as the judicial rules will be shaped by how the prosecutor exercises his original charging authority, but also that prosecutions will on occasion be compelled. Overall, however, the objective should not be to deny discretion to the prosecutor but rather to require that he share with the courts a responsibility for the public interest in criminal law.

We must somehow resist the suggestion that our courts are so overworked that it is impossible to frame a dialogue between judge and prosecutor which will move our legal system towards greater rationality. It does not serve the cause of legality to permit officials to ignore the legislature, or to have legislatures act on the assumption that their statutes will be ignored or discounted. It does not serve the cause of correction to have prosecutors spare judges the pain of making appropriate decisions by labeling charges incorrectly. And it is not genuinely helpful to prosecutors to burden them with so heavy a responsibility for defining and administering criminal law. If we can tame the prosecutor's discretion, allowing him latitude while requiring adherence to rules, we would have a clearer sense of what crimes are being committed, who comprises our offender population, and the theories underlying charging and disposition. We would then be in a better position to deal with more fundamental problems —the undue use of criminal law as a regulatory instrument, an overly fragmented and decentralized system of criminal justice, sentences so severe and offenses so redundant and overlapping that they create too much pressure on the legal system—on one hand bending that system's provisions in the direction of leniency and discretion, on the other inviting arbitrary and unequal administration and trivializing the rule of law.[27]

NOTES

Introduction

1. See generally Frank W. Miller, *Prosecution: The Decision To Charge a Suspect with a Crime* (Boston: Little, Brown, 1969); Donald J. Newman, *Conviction: The Determination of Guilt or Innocence Without Trial* (Boston: Little, Brown, 1966); David W. Neubauer, *Criminal Justice in Middle America* (North Scituate, Mass.: Duxbury Press, 1974), 42 et seq. See also the discussion of United States v. Batchelder, 442 U.S. 114 (1979), in Comment, "Duplicative Statutes, Prosecutorial Discretion, and the Illinois Armed Violence Statute," 71 *J. Crim. L. & Crimin.* 226 (1980).
2. Virtually nowhere is the district attorney part of a state department of justice. Though each state has an attorney general, his authority does not ordinarily extend to criminal matters. See Note, "Circumventing the Corrupt Prosecutor," 48 *J. Crim. L. & Crimin.* 531 (1958). See also Malcolm M. Feeley, "Two Models of the Criminal Justice System: An Organizational Perspective," 7 *Law & Soc. Rev.* 407, 422 (1973), who describes the criminal justice system as possessing "virtually no instruments to supervise practices and secure compliance to the formal goals of the organization." As to the federal system, see Charles F. C. Ruff, "Federal Prosecution of Local Corruption: A Case Study in the Making of Law Enforcement Policy," 65 *Geo L. J.* 1171, 1201–8 (1977).
3. On the distinction between accusatorial and inquisitorial systems, see Abraham S. Goldstein, "Reflections on Two Models: Inquisitorial Themes in American Criminal Procedure," 26 *Stan. L. Rev.* 1009 (1974); Mirjan Damaska, "Evidentiary Barriers to Conviction and Two Models of Criminal Procedure: A Comparative Study," 121 *U. Pa. L. Rev.* 506 (1973). On private prosecution in England, see J. L. J. Edwards, *Law Officers of the Crown* (London: Sweet & Maxwell, 1964),

c. 16. The American prosecutor has even more of a monopoly of the charging power than do prosecutors in "inquisitorial" systems. Our victim may never prosecute directly and he may not join as a *partie civile,* as in France. See A. V. Sheehan, *Criminal Procedure in Scotland and France* (Edinburgh: Her Majesty's Stationary Office, 1975), 20–23. See generally Abraham S. Goldstein and Martin Marcus, "The Myth of Judicial Supervision in Three Inquisitorial Systems: France, Italy, and Germany," 87 *Yale L. J.* 240 (1977).

4. See Jerome Hall, *General Principles of Criminal Law* (2nd ed; Indianapolis: Bobbs-Merrill, 1960), c.2; Arthur Bonfield, "The Abrogation of Penal Statutes by Nonenforcement," 49 *Ia. L. Rev.* 389 (1964); Paul Gewirtz, "The Courts, Congress and Executive Policy Making," 46 *Law & Contemp. Prob.* 46, 73–4 (1976).

5. On the exlusionary rule, see Mapp v. Ohio, 367 U.S. 643 (1961); on plain error, see Chapman v. California, 386 U.S. 18 (1967); on counsel, see Gideon v. Wainwright, 372 U.S. 335 (1963). For cases illustrating judicial attention to methods of investigation, see Abraham S. Goldstein and Leonard Orland, *Criminal Procedure: Cases and Materials on the Administration of Criminal Law* (Boston: Little, Brown, 1974), c. 9–11.

6. Young v. United States, 315 U.S. 257, 258–59 (1942).

7. See Owen M. Fiss, *The Civil Rights Injunction* (Bloomington: Indiana University Press, 1978); Abram Chayes, "The Role of the Judge in Public Law Litigation," 89 *Harv. L. Rev.* 1281 (1976); Nathan Glazer, "Towards an Imperial Judiciary?" *Public Interest* No. 41 (Fall, 1975), 104; Note, "The Wyatt Case: Implementation of a Judicial Decree Ordering Institutional Change," 84 *Yale L. J.* 1338 (1975).

8. As an adversary, the prosecutor is inclined to make only limited disclosure of the evidence that he (and the grand jury) have gathered against the defendant. A network of rules supports him in that inclination. At the same time, he is obligated to serve "justice" and turn exculpatory evidence over to the defendant. Brady v. Maryland, 373 U.S. 83, 87 (1963).

9. Coolidge v. New Hampshire, 403 U.S. 443, 449 (1971), quoting Johnson v. United States, 333 U.S. 10, 13–14 (1948). See also State v. Simpson, 137 N.W. 2d 391 (Wis. 1965) (The district attorney is not "the equivalent of a neutral and detached magistrate who may constitutionally be empowered to authorize the issuance of the [arrest] warrant."); Imbler v. Pachtman, 424 U.S. 409, 431 (1976) ("At some point, with respect to some decisions, the prosecutor no doubt functions as an administrator rather than as an officer of the court. Drawing a proper line between these functions may present difficult questions").

10. Gerstein v. Pugh, 420 U.S. 103 (1975).

I.

1. The relevant federal statute, 28 U.S.C. § 547(1) (1968), provides: "Except as otherwise provided by law, each United States Attorney, within his district, shall—(1) prosecute for all offenses against the United States." The statutes of many states are similar. None confer discretion in explicit terms. See, *e.g.*, New York County Laws § 700(1) (McKinney, 1972); Ill. Rev. Stat., Chap. 14, § 5 (1969). For a typical discussion of the prosecutor's discretion under the federal statute, see Pugach v. Klein, 193 F.Supp. 630, 634–35 (S.D.N.Y. 1961).
2. State v. Winne, 96 A.2d 63, 72 (N.J. 1953) (Otherwise, "an honest but negligent prosecutor would have it within his power to cripple or nullify the enforcement of the criminal law in his county or to choose at his pleasure the portion of the criminal law he would enforce. He would have . . . the suspending power sought so strenuously by Stuart Kings . . . but denied to them in the English Bill of Rights. . . . There is no difference in principle . . . between a Stuart openly defying and preventing the execution of the law and a county prosecutor winking at and tolerating the violation of the laws").
3. 468 F.2d 389 (7th Cir. 1972), rev'd in part on other grounds, sub nom. O'Shea v. Littleton, 414 U.S. 488, remanded in part on other grounds sub. nom. Spomer v. Littleton, 414 U.S. 514 (1974).
4. The principal Supreme Court decision denying standing is Linda R. S. v. Richard D. et al, 410 U.S. 614, 619 (1973), in which the mother of an illegitimate child asked a Texas district attorney to prosecute the father because he had not supported the child. The district attorney refused because he construed the child support law as applicable only to fathers of legitimate children. Justice Marshall, for the Court, said Linda R. S. lacked "standing" because she had failed to allege "a direct nexus between the vindication of her interest and the enforcement of the State's criminal laws." As a private citizen, she did not have a "judicially cognizable interest in the prosecution or non-prosecution of another." The cases suggesting that "standing" might exist are Inmates of Attica Correctional Facility v. Rockefeller, 477 F.2d 375, 378 (2nd Cir. 1973) (denying plaintiffs' request for a writ of mandamus to compel prosecution of state officials for criminal acts arising out of the Attica prison uprising. Standing might exist if prison inmates were in danger of sustaining injury by virtue of nonenforcement of the criminal law against state officials); Nader v. Saxbe, 497 F.2d 676, 679 n.18, 19, and 681 n.27 (D.C. Cir. 1974) (Ralph Nader sought to compel prosecution for violation of the campaign election law, alleging that there had been only one prosecution under the act and that the policy of nonenforcement had nullified the law, fostered dishonesty in elec-

tions, and deprived him and other voters of information about the candidates. The district court dismissed the complaint. On appeal, the court upheld the dismissal as moot, but noted that a policy of nonenforcement differed from an "essentially executive" decision on prosecuting a particular person and was reviewable).

5. 118 U.S. 356, 373–74 (1886).
6. 368 U.S. 448, 456 (1962).
7. In Oyler v. Boles, *ibid.*, Oyler asserted in a petition for habeas corpus that he was the only one, among 904 offenders eligible for a mandatory life sentence under a habitual criminal law, who had been charged as an habitual offender. The Supreme Court noted that the "conscious exercise of some selectivity in enforcement is not in itself a federal constitutional violation." The Court did not make explicit the extent to which irrational enforcement practices might be regarded as "arbitrary" even if they did not involve race or religion, though Oyler itself, which involved neither, offered some indication of what might qualify. See United States v. Batchelder, 442 U.S. 114 (1979) (in absence of discrimination against a class of individuals, the prosecutor is free to elect the more severe of two overlapping statutes in bringing an indictment).
8. City of Minneapolis v. Buschette, 240 N.W. 2d 500, 505 (Minn. 1976).
9. In addition to United States v. Falk, 479 F.2d 616 (7th Cir. 1973), see United States v. Steele, 461 F.2d 1148, 1151–52 (9th Cir. 1972) ("Steele demonstrated a purposeful discrimination by census authorities against those who had publicly expressed their opinions about the census. . . . [T]he government was required to explain it away, if possible, by showing the selection process actually rested upon some valid ground. Mere random selection would suffice, since the government is not obligated to prosecute all offenders"); United States v. Crowthers, 456 F.2d 1074, 1078, 1080 (4th Cir. 1972) (prosecution had to prove that disorderly conduct charges were not brought because the defendants had assembled before the Pentagon to say "Masses for Peace"); Dixon v. District of Columbia, 394 F.2d 966 (D.C. Cir. 1968); United States v. Berrios, 501 F.2d 1207 (2nd Cir. 1974). The defense was denied in the following non-First Amendment cases: Butler v. Cooper, 554 F.2d 645 (4th Cir. 1977) (fact that 98 percent of arrests for liquor law violations were of black persons was insufficient to show racially discriminatory enforcement); United States v. Kelly, 556 F.2d 257 (5th Cir. 1977), cert. den. 434 U.S. 1017 (1978); United States v. Johnson, 577 F.2d 1304 (5th Cir. 1978).
10. 479 F.2d, 620–21, 623–24.
11. See, *e.g.*, Rule 16(b) of the *Federal Rules of Criminal Procedure* (excluding from discovery "reports, memoranda, or other internal govern-

ment documents made by the attorney for the government or other government agents in connection with the investigation or prosecution of a case"); United States v. Agurs, 427 U.S. 97 (1976); but see United States v. Berrios, 501 F.2d 1207, 1211 (2nd Cir. 1974). The *Falk* majority said that a defendant cannot be denied an opportunity "to prove that the prosecution stems from an improper prosecutorial design or . . . [to] question a prosecutor under oath" but noted that it would ordinarily be improper to question a prosecutor as to his motives. United States v. Falk, 479 F.2d at 620. To the dissenters it would be "the ultimate transgression of judicial authority to haul the executive to the witness stand for examination by a criminal defendant as to why it has chosen to indict him." 479 F.2d at 630. When a judge seeks information in order to rule on a motion to dismiss, the matter is arguably distinguishable from the usual discovery situation. In asking for an exercise of judicial discretion, the prosecutor should be obligated to show the judge the facts on which his decision is to be based. Protective orders of the sort authorized by Rule 16(d)(1) could be used to insure that sensitive information would be protected. And the prosecutor, who initiated the motion, can prevent even *in camera* disclosure by withdrawing it.

12. Note, "Nolle Prosequi," 1958 *Crim. L. Rev. (Eng.)* 573, 574. Today, the *nolle prosequi* is used hardly at all in England. Its function of public control of prosecutions instituted by private parties has been taken over by the director of public prosecutions, who is authorized by statute to assume direction of virtually any case. The great bulk of private prosecutions is now brought by the police.
13. National Commission on Law Observance and Enforcement, *Report on Prosecution* (Washington, D. C.: Government Printing Office, 1931), 19; see People ex rel Elliott v. Covelli, 112 N.E. 2d 156, 158–60 (Ill. 1953).
14. 2 Mass. 172 (1806) (holding that a *nolle* entered on one indictment is no bar to a second indictment for the same offense).
15. 74 U.S. 454, 457 (1868).
16. Joseph H. Beale, *Criminal Pleading and Practice* (Boston: Little, Brown, 1899), 344–45 ("at present any official prosecuting attorney has power to enter it, at least by leave of court," citing P. v. McLeod, 1 Hill 377, 405).
17. State v. Tufts, 56 N.H. 137, 139 (1875).
18. State v. Thompson, 10 N.C. (3 Hawks) 613, 614 (1825). See also State v. Moody, 69 N.C. 529, 531 (1871); Denham v. Robinson, 77 S.E. 970, 971–72 (W.Va. 1913).
19. Roscoe Pound, *Criminal Justice in America* (New York: H. Holt, 1930), 185.

20. William Gemmill, "What Is Wrong with the Administration of Our Criminal Laws?" 4 *J. of Amer. Inst. of Crim. L. & Crimin.* 698, 703 (1913).
21. People v. Newcomer, 120 N.E. 244, 247 (Ill. 1918).
22. Pound, *Criminal Justice in America,* 187. See Sam B. Warner and Henry B. Cabot, "Changes in the Administration of Criminal Justice During the Past Fifty Years," 50 *Harv. L. Rev.* 583, 597–98 (1937).
23. See state statutes outlined in American Law Institute, *Code of Criminal Procedure,* Commentary to Section 295 (Philadelphia: American Law Institute, 1930), 895–97.
24. The California statute of 1850, which subsequently became § 1385, is quoted in People v. More, 12 Pac. 631, 632 (Cal. 1887). For a fuller discussion of the California practice, see People v. Superior Court (Howard), 446 P.2d 138, 145 et seq. (Cal. 1968). *Cf.* People v. Quill, 177 N.Y.S. 2d 380, 381 (Kings County Ct. 1958) (Under a "statutory enactment of the former power of *nolle prosequi*", the court has "sole discretion to dismiss an indictment in the interest of justice" and the district attorney's consent is not necessary). In Connecticut, the court said that judges have "no inherent power to dismiss a case in the furtherance of justice," setting aside a trial judge's entry of a guilty plea to a lesser offense entered over the prosecutor's objection. State v. Carr, 376 A.2d 74, 76 (Conn. 1977).
25. People v. Tenorio, 473 P.2d 993, 996 (Cal. 1970), overruling People v. Sidener, 375 P.2d 641 (Cal. 1962), cert. den. 374 U.S. 494 (1963), in which Chief Justice Roger Traynor had written that judicial discretion over dismissals was created by the legislature and could be modified by it to remove punitive consequences of narcotic recidivism. See also People v. Burke, 301 P.2d 241, 244–45 (Cal. 1956).
26. People v. Superior Court (Fellman), 130 Cal. Rptr. 548, 522 (App. 2nd Dist. 1976). See also State v. Leonardis, 375 A.2d 607 (N.J. 1977) (discussing judicial review of "diversion" from prosecution).
27. People v. Superior Court (King), 57 Cal. Rptr. 892, 895 (App. 1st Dist. 1967).
28. People v. Orin, 533 P.2d 193, 199 et seq. (Cal. 1975).
29. People v. Tanner, 156 Cal. Rptr. 450, 452 n.3, 596 P.2d 328, 330 (en banc, 1979).
30. United States v. Brokaw, 60 F.Supp. 100 (S.D. Ill. 1945); United States v. Woody, 2 F.2d 262 (D. Mont. 1924). See Confiscation Cases, 118 U.S. at 373–74; but *cf.* United States v. Krakowitz, 52 F.Supp. 774, 784 (S.D. Ohio, 1943).
31. Rule 48(a), *Federal Rules of Criminal Procedure.* For the background of the rule, see Lester B. Orfield, *Criminal Procedure Under the Federal Rules* (6 vols.; Rochester, N.Y.: Lawyers Co-operative, 1967),

VI, 336–43; Leon Yankwich, "Increasing Judicial Discretion in Criminal Proceedings," 1 F.R.D. 746, 747–52 (1941).

32. 101 F.Supp. 609 (D. Conn. 1951).
33. 168 F.Supp. 225, 229–230 (D. Ind. 1958).
34. United States v. Greater Blouse, Skirt & Neckwear Contractors Association, 228 F.Supp. 483, 486–87 (S.D.N.Y. 1964). Whether Judge Weinfeld meant that these are the only proper justifications for dismissal under the rule, as was suggested in *Doe,* is not clear. A footnote, *id.,* 487 n.12, cites *Shanahan*'s holding that prejudice to the government in another prosecution may be an adequate justification. Moore lists six possible reasons for dismissing a prosecution, other than insufficiency of proof: "death of the defendant, incurable insanity or incompetency to stand trial, serious and incurable physical disease or disability, defendant a fugitive, protection of government security against possible trial disclosures, and the superseding of the indictment." James W. Moore, *Federal Practice* (2nd ed.; 12 vols.; Albany: Matthew Bender, 1979), VIII B, § 48.02(2).
35. 228 F.Supp., 489–90. The opinion leaves unclear whether the court "would be without power" to deny dismissal only when the dismissal is based on evidentiary or harassment grounds, or whether its lack of power would also extend to dismissals based on enforcement policy considerations—*e.g.,* those made as part of plea negotiations or to reward "cooperative" defendants.
36. Charles A. Wright, *Federal Practice and Procedure* (3 vols.; St. Paul, Minn.: West, 1969), III, § 812, p. 305, quoted in Comment to Rule 231(h), *Uniform Rules of Criminal Procedure* (St. Paul, Minn.: West, 1974), 52. Rule 231 provides: "The prosecuting attorney may dismiss the information or any count thereof by filing a notice of the dismissal. The notice shall state the reasons for the dismissal."
37. 342 F.2d 167, 171, 172 (5th Cir. 1965), cert. den. 381 U.S. 935 (1965).
38. 342 F.2d at 179.
39. 381 F.Supp. 214, 222–23 (N.D. Tex. 1974).
40. 396 F.Supp. 803, 804–5 (N.D. Tex. 1974). In appointing a special prosecutor, Judge Hill was drawing upon a relatively sparse body of precedent that found appointing authority in statutes explicitly addressed to the problem or in the court's "inherent powers." The typical statutes provide for court appointment when the regular government attorney is absent, is disqualified because of interest, or refuses to perform his duties. See generally Note, "The Special Prosecutor in the Federal System," 11 *Am. Crim. L. Rev.* 577, 579 (1973); Note, "The Proposed Court-Appointed Special Prosecutor," 87 *Yale L. J.* 1692 (1978). As to inherent power, see State ex rel Clyde v. Lauder, 90 N.W. 564, 569 (N.D. 1902); Taylor v. State, 38 So. 380 (Fla. 1905); Forsythe v. Coate,

546 P.2d 1060 (Mont. 1976). The New Jersey Supreme Court had earlier noted that its statute authorizing appointment of a special prosecutor would withstand attack as violative of separation of powers "if the totality of circumstances were such as to indicate a wilfully significant violation clearly calling for prosecution." In re Ringwood Fact Finding Comm., 324 A.2d 1, 4 (N.J. 1974); but *cf.* People v. Municipal Court (Siple), 103 Cal. Rptr. 645, 656 (App. 2nd Dist. 1972) (appellate court vacated appointment of a private attorney to conduct prosecution after the district attorney refused to file complaint); Murphy v. Yates, 348 A.2d 837 (Md. App. 1975) (statute creating a statewide special prosecutor was held invalid as divesting states attorneys of part of their common-law power to prosecute).

41. United States v. Cowan, 524 F.2d 504, 512–15 (5th Cir. 1975), cert. den. 425 U.S. 971 (1976). In Rinaldi v. United States, 434 U.S. 22, 29–30 n.15 (1978), the Supreme Court commented on the role of the court under Rule 48(a) of the *Federal Rules of Criminal Procedure*:

> The words 'leave of court' were inserted in Rule 48(a) without explanation. While they obviously vest some discretion in the court, the circumstances in which that discretion may properly be exercised have not been delineated by this court. The principal object . . . is apparently to protect a defendant against prosecutorial harassment, e.g. charging, dismissing, and recharging when the Government moves to dismiss an indictment over the defendant's objection. . . . But the Rule has also been held to permit the court to deny a Government dismissal motion to which the defendant has consented if the motion is prompted by considerations clearly contrary to the public interest [citing *Cowan* and *Ammidown*]. It is unnecessary to decide whether the court has discretion under these circumstances, since, even assuming it does, the result in the case remains the same.

Rinaldi reversed *In re Washington*, 531 F.2d 297, 302, aff'd en banc, 544 F.2d 203, 207–9 (5th Cir. 1976), in which the Fifth Circuit upheld a trial judge's denial of the government's motion for dismissal after conviction. The motion was based on the ground that the defendant had already been convicted of state charges arising out of the same incident and that it was the policy of the Justice Department [under Petite v. United States, 361 U.S. 529 (1960)] not to try a defendant on federal charges in such cases. The trial and appellate courts concluded that the government had abused its authority and "manipulated" the judiciary because it had known of the state prosecution during the federal trial and had persisted until conviction because it feared the state conviction would be reversed. For other cases denying the government motion to dismiss, see United States v. M.V. Nederlandische Combinatie, 428 F.Supp. 114, 117 (S.D.N.Y. 1977) (rejecting dismissal when

(1) "government does not contend that insufficient evidence exists" but only that prosecution "would be at great public expense without any certainty of success due to the difficulty in gathering witnesses and the possible frailty of witness' memory," and (2) refusing to be "privy to any agreement by which some defendants entered guilty pleas in return for dismissals as to others"); United States v. Biddings, 416 F.Supp. 673, 675 (E.D. Ill. 1976) (refusing to accept dismissal on the basis of newly discovered evidence after conviction of kidnapping; "it would delegate to the prosecutor the right to decide between conflicting evidence and make a mockery of the grand jury system . . . if this indictment is abandoned"); United States v. Robins, 426 F.Supp. 1221, 1224 (S.D.N.Y. 1976).

Cf. United States v. Olson, 504 F.2d 1222, 1225 (9th Cir. 1974) (though trial court had commendable motives in seeking to deal with prosecutorial policy of presenting to the grand jury a lengthy multiple-count indictment that burdened an "already over busy" court, such motives did not justify an invasion of the powers of the executive. Court was not authorized to order government to elect one count for trial and then, upon failure of government to do so, to dismiss indictment with prejudice. "On the District Attorney rests the responsibility to determine whether to prosecute, when to prosecute, and on what charges to prosecute. A case is not to be summarily dismissed because it disagrees with some policy of the District Attorney's office"); United States v. Gainey, 440 F.2d 290 (D.C. Cir. 1971) (dismissal over government objection to reduce backlog is invalid); United States v. Real, 446 F.2d 40 (9th Cir. 1971) (reversing a dismissal by the trial judge in the interest of justice. "The district court's merciful inclinations appear entirely appropriate in view of the nature of the offense, of Eck's youth. . . . However, we are unable to find any authority permitting judicial discretion to be substituted for prosecutorial discretion in dismissing the indictment"); United States v. DeDiego, 511 F.2d 818, 824 (D.C. Cir. 1975) ("A trial judge has no discretion to end prosecutions unless there are legal grounds for the exercise of discretion"); United States v. Bettinger Corp., 54 *F.R.D.* 40 (D. Mass. 1971) (rejected, as a basis for dismissal by the court, the defendant's current compliance with the ecology laws allegedly violated.)

The American Law Institute's *Model Penal Code* would authorize a judge to dismiss an offense under defined circumstances which make the offense a *de minimis* violation. *Model Penal Code* (St. Paul, Minn.: West, 1974), § 2.12, p. 475. See also the proposal to amend Rule 48(a) to authorize the federal court to dismiss "if . . . it concludes that such proposal will serve the ends of justice and the effective administration of the court's business." "Preliminary Draft of Proposed Amendments to the Federal Rules of Criminal Procedure," 48 F.R.D. 553, 640 (1970).

42. 29 Neb. Rev. Stat. § 1606 (1975). A similar Michigan statute provides that the prosecutor must state his reasons for not filing an information, and that "the court may examine such statement together with the evidence filed in the case and if, upon such examination, the court shall not be satisfied with said statement, the prosecuting attorney shall be directed by the court to file the proper information and bring the case to trial." *Michigan Compiled Laws Annotated* (St. Paul, Minn.: West, 1968), § 767.41, as amended 1978 (Supp. 1980).

43. The Colorado statute was said in Tooley v. District Court, 549 P.2d 772 (Colo. 1976), to allow the appointment of a special prosecutor only upon a finding of "abuse of discretion" and a finding of "clear and convincing evidence that the terms of the statute had been met." The court emphasized that the trial judge "should not substitute his judgment or discretion for that of the prosecutor in the case and vacated" the appointment of a special prosecutor upon finding no abuse of discretion in the prosecutor's refusal to prosecute because the victim had originally declined to cooperate.

44. See State v. Leonardis, 375 A.2d 607 (N.J. 1977); but see Anderson v. Haas, 602 P.2d 346 (Ore. 1979).

45. See Leonard W. Levy, *Origins of the Fifth Amendment* (New York: Oxford University Press, 1968), 359, 384–86.

46. *Model State Witness Immunity Act* (St. Paul, Minn.: West, 1957), 190. This objective is carried out in the act in one of two ways. The first treats the prosecutor and the attorney general as "the enforcement authority," with the latter serving as "a check against hasty or improper action, [and] to provide a broad view of the enforcement situation as corrective to the views of local prosecutors." *Id.*, 191. The role of the court is limited to assuring observance of procedural requirements. The second alternative places reliance primarily on the prosecutor, creating what is plainly a presumption favoring court approval of requests that the prosecutor alone may initiate. It "is intended for use when neither the Attorney General nor any other comparable official serves as central coordinating officer for the enforcement of state criminal law . . . [and] should serve as a salutary check against the possible overzealousness, unwisdom, or corruption of local prosecutors." *Id.*, 192. See generally, Comment, "State Immunity Statutes in Constitutional Perspective," 1968 *Duke L. J.* 311; Note, "Witness Immunity Statutes," 51 *Boston U. L. Rev.* 616 (1971); Comment, "The Fifth Amendment and Compelled Testimony," 19 *Vill. L. Rev.* 470 (1974).

47. *United States Statutes at Large,* Act of Aug. 20, 1954, 68 Stat. 745 (83d Cong., 2d Sess), which became 18 U.S.C. § 3486. In 1968, 18 U.S.C. § 2514 was enacted and was patterned on the 1954 statute, as is the current immunity statute, enacted in 1970 and amended in 1973, 18 U.S.C. § 6001 et seq. (1973). The House Report accompanying the 1973 bill noted, "The court's role . . . is merely to find the facts on which the order is predicated. . . . Review that second judges prosecutive discretion is not authorized." "Federal Immunity of Witnesses Act," *House Reports,* 91–1188, to accompany H.R. 11157, 91st Cong., 2d Sess. (1970), 13.
48. *House Reports,* 2606, Aug. 3, 1954, quoted in 2 *U.S. Code Congressional and Administrative News* (St. Paul, Minn.: West, 1954). Congressman Keating noted on the floor of Congress that an immunity order would be issued by a judge only "if [he were] convinced of . . . [its] propriety." 100 *Congressional Record* 13323 (H. Rep., 93rd Cong., 1st Sess., Aug. 4, 1954).
49. Ullman v. United States, 350 U.S. 422, 432–33 (1956). In construing the Immunity Act of 1954 as denying such discretion, the Court noted that to do otherwise would "raise a serious constitutional question as to the role of the judiciary under the doctrine of separation of powers."
50. In re Bart, 304 F.2d 631, 635 (D.C. Cir. 1962). See also In re Russo, 448 F.2d 369, 372 (9th Cir. 1971).
51. Informal immunity may surface when the prosecutor informs the court that there are other offenses that could be charged against the defendant and that should be taken into consideration in sentencing.
52. Donald J. Newman, *Conviction: The Determination of Guilt or Innocence Without Trial* (Boston: Little, Brown, 1969), 187.
53. United States v. Ford, 99 U.S. 594, 598 (1878), commonly referred to as the "Whiskey Cases."
54. *Id.,* 606. See the earlier opinions in People v. Whipple, 9 Cowen 707 (Oyer & Terminer, N.Y. 1827); Comm. v. Knapp, 10 Pick. 477 (Mass. 1830); United States v. Lee, Fed. Cas. No. 15,588 (C.C.A. Ill. 1846) ("The government is bound in honor . . . to carry out the understanding . . . by which the witness testified, and admitted, in so doing, his own turpitude. . . . If the district attorney shall fail to enter a nolle prosequi . . . the court will continue the cause until an application can be made for a pardon. The court would suggest that to discontinue the prosecution is the shorter and better mode)"; People v. Groves, 219 Pac. 1033, 1035 (Cal. App. 1923) ("If the district attorney made such representations . . . he clearly exceeded his authority insofar as binding his own office or the court is concerned"). And see State v. Brown, 321 A.2d 478, 484 (Me. 1974) ("Any alternative attempt to grant immunity and compel testimony without complying with the . . . [statutory] for-

malities . . . is without legal authority. . . . There is no inherent authority within the office of a prosecuting attorney to grant immunity to a witness"); Comm. v. Carrera, 227 A.2d 627, 630 (Pa. 1967); Hunter v. United States, 405 F.2d 1187, 1188 (9th Cir. 1969); Appl. of Parham, 431 P.2d 86, 88 (Ariz. 1967); but see United States v. Levy, 153 F.2d 995, 997 (3rd Cir. 1946).

55. 177 N.E. 489, 495 (N.Y. 1931).
56. 108 Cal. Rptr. 501 (App. 2nd Dist. 1973), discussed in Comment, "Judicial Supervision of Non-Statutory Immunity," 65 *J. Crim. L. & Crimin.* 334 (1974).
57. 108 Cal. Rptr. at 506, 507.
58. United States v. Carter, 454 F.2d 426, 428 (4th Cir. 1972), cert. den. 417 U.S. 933.
59. 404 U.S. 257, 262 (1971). It might be argued that *Santobello* is distinguishable because New York prosecutors are explicitly authorized to make sentence recommendations but not to promise immunity. Nevertheless, a prosecutor would seem to have apparent authority to promise immunity, and defendants are presumably entitled to rely on that apparent authority. After *Santobello*, the Fourth Circuit added a postscript to its *Carter* opinion, asserting that its view of the law had now been supported by the Supreme Court. See also In re Snoonian, 502 F.2d 110, 112 (1st Cir. 1974); United States v. Corrale, 479 F.2d 944 (1st Cir. 1973).
60. Testimony of Richard Green, deputy director, National Commission on Reform of Federal Criminal Code, Hearings before the Sub-Committee on Criminal Laws and Procedures of the Committee on the Judiciary, U.S. Senate, *Measures Relating to Organized Crime*, 91st Cong., 1st Sess. (1969), 327.

II.

1. See generally Donald J. Newman, *Conviction: The Decision to Charge a Suspect with a Crime* (Boston: Little, Brown, 1969); Abraham S. Blumberg, *Criminal Justice* (Chicago: Quadrangle, 1967); Milton Heuman, *Plea Bargaining: The Experiences of Prosecutors, Judges, and Defense Attorneys* (Chicago: Univ. of Chicago Press, 1978); Albert W. Alschuler, "Plea Bargaining and Its History," 79 *Col. L. Rev.* 1 (1979); Note, "Guilty Plea Bargaining: Compromises by Prosecutors to Secure Guilty Pleas," 112 *U. Pa. L. Rev.* 865 (1964); Note, "The Unconstitutionality of Plea Bargaining," 83 *Harv. L. Rev.* 1387 (1970). And see the Court's comment in Blackledge v. Allison, 431 U.S. 63, 76 (1977) ("For decades it was a *sub rosa* process shrouded in secrecy and deliberately concealed by participating defendants, defense lawyers, prosecutors,

and even judges"). Cases illustrating the general position are State v. Keep, 166 Pac. 936, 938 (Ore. 1919) ("only misdemeanors may be compromised"); State v. D'Autremont, 317 P.2d 932, 935 (Ore. 1957); State v. Lopez, 19 Mo. 254 (1853); but see State v. Ward, 165 S.E. 803, 804 (W.Va. 1932).

2. 397 U.S. 742, 753 (1970) ("we cannot hold that it is unconstitutional for the State to extend a benefit to a defendant who in turn extends a substantial benefit to the State and who demonstrates by his plea that he is ready and willing to admit his crime and to enter the correctional system in a frame of mind that affords hope for success in rehabilitation over a shorter period of time than might otherwise be necessary." The Court noted, in addition, that "a contrary holding . . . [would make it] necessary to forbid prosecutors and judges to accept guilty pleas to selected counts, to lesser included offenses, or to reduced charges. The Fifth Amendment does not reach so far."). Earlier opinions had dealt explicitly with structurally induced pleas without referring to negotiated pleas.
3. *Id.*, 754.
4. 400 U.S 25 (1970)
5. 404 U.S. 257, 262 (1971)
6. Cooper v. United States, 594 F.2d 12, 18–19 (4th Cir. 1979) (where the prosecutor's superior vetoed his offer before defense counsel accepted, original offer remained binding as long as circumstances had not changed.)
7. 397 U.S., 755. In Shelton v. United States, 242 F.2d 101, rev'd en banc, 246 F.2d 571 (5th Cir. 1957), rev'd 356 U.S. 26 (1958), defendant claimed his guilty plea was involuntary because it was induced by the promise of the assistant United States attorney that he would receive a sentence of only one year. In *Brady*, the Supreme Court relied on the en banc opinion (Shelton II) that was written by Judge Tuttle. The first opinion will be referred to hereafter in notes as Shelton I. Note that Shelton II was reversed by the Supreme Court as a result of a confession of error by the solicitor general that the guilty plea "may have been improperly obtained."
8. *Id.*, 751 n.8.
9. *Id.*, 758
10. The quoted words are from the majority opinion in Shelton I, 242 F.2d, 113.
11. See Judge Tuttle's dissent in Shelton I, 242 F.2d, 113 et seq., which became the majority view in Shelton II, 246 F.2d 571 (5th Cir. 1957).
12. 434 U.S. 357 (1978). *Cf.* Corbitt v. New Jersey, 439 U.S. 212, 221 (1978); United States v. Paglia, 190 F.2d 445 (2nd Cir. 1951) (Judge Learned Hand held that when the government has overcharged and

then drops a count which it could not have proved, the dropped charge cannot constitute "valid consideration" for a guilty plea).

13. See Donald J. Newman, "The Agnew Plea Bargain," 10 *Crim. L. Bull.* 85, 88 (1974) ("Is it proper for a prosecutor—fully aware that he has a weak case, to negotiate a plea in order to assure conviction when he is 'morally certain' an offender is guilty, though unlikely to be convicted? Suppose . . . the prosecutor ends up with no admissible evidence . . . but the defendant is unaware of this?"); Herbert S. Miller, William F. McDonald, and James A. Cramer, *Plea Bargaining in the United States* (Washington, D.C.: National Institute of Law Enforcement and Criminal Justice, 1978), 116 ("Judges have not seen the supervision of bluffing as falling within the purview of their function. They are aware that bluffing occurs").

14. Rule 11(e)(1) of the *Federal Rules of Criminal Procedure* provides that the charge may be reduced to a lesser or related offense; the government may promise to move for dismissal of other charges; the government may agree to recommend or not to oppose a particular sentence; the government and defense attorney may agree on a given sentence. The status of a plea agreement requiring a defendant to cooperate with the government is more ambiguous. See Note, "Rule 11 and Collateral Attack on Guilty Pleas," 86 *Yale L. J.* 1395, 1404 n.36 (1977). For discussion of undue pressure used by prosecutor to persuade defendant to abandon his claim to dismissal for denial of a speedy trial, as a prerequisite to being permitted to plead guilty to a lesser offense, see People v. Blakley, 313 N.E. 2d 763, 764–65 (N.Y. 1974); People v. White, 298 N.E. 2d 659, 664 (N.Y. 1973). For cases dealing with use of a threat to charge a third person if defendant does not acknowledge his guilt, see People v. James, 217 N.W. 2d 408, 410 (Mich. Ct. App. 1974), remanded for evidentiary hearing, 225 N.W. 2d 520 (Mich. 1975); People v. Duran, 498 P.2d 937 (Colo. 1972); Crow v. United States, 397 F.2d 284, 285 (10th Cir. 1968) and Kent v. United States, 272 F.2d 795, 798 (1st Cir. 1959). The American Law Institute originally voted to prohibit any prosecutorial promise of leniency to a third person, but it deleted the ban from the final draft of its *Model Code of Pre-Arraignment Procedure*. American Law Institute, *Model Code of Pre-Arraignment Procedure* (Tentative Draft, 1972), 5, 106. The ALI Reporter believes that such inducements should be prohibited because they may cause an innocent man to plead guilty and/or because the defendant "will receive treatment that does not meet his correctional needs and that he does not deserve in terms of his own character and dangerousness." On unfulfillable promises, see Palermo v. Warden, Green Haven State Prison, 545 F.2d 286, 296 (2nd Cir. 1976) ("The reasoning underlying *Santobello* applies no less when the prosecutor makes unfulfillable prom-

ises in negotiating a plea." The district attorney had promised parole action beyond his authority); Geisser v. United States, 513 F.2d 862 (5th Cir. 1975).

15. Rule 11(d), *Federal Rules of Criminal Procedure*; McCarthy v. United States, 394 U.S. 459, 467 (1966); Boykin v. Alabama, 395 U.S. 238 (1969).

16. See Tollett v. Henderson, 411 U.S. 258 (1973); Michael Tigar, "Foreword: Waiver of Constitutional Rights: Disquiet in the Citadel," 84 *Harv. L. Rev.* 1 (1970); Albert W. Alschuler, "The Trial Judge's Role in Plea Bargaining, Part I," 76 *Col. L. Rev.* 1059, 1065–66 (1976); Raymond I. Parnas and Riley J. Atkins, "Abolishing Plea Bargaining: A Proposal," 14 *Crim. L. Bull.* 101, 118 (1978):

> Many people presently plead guilty for reasons unconnected with prosecutorial concessions made during bargaining. Some defendants desire immediate punishment as a perceived absolution for their crimes. Others plead to eliminate the uncertainty and anxiety of not knowing what the inauspicious future holds. Some desire to avoid the inevitable expense of lengthening and delaying the process. Others seek to forestall embarrassment to themselves, family and friends precipitated by a trial. It is not uncommon for some to plead to move on quickly from a less favorable place of confinement to a more favorable one. The possibility of probation or sentencing to time served are further enticements to a plea of guilty.

17. Rule 11(f), *Federal Rules of Criminal Procedure*, 18 U.S.C.A. and Supp. (1980). Rule 11(e)(1) provides that a plea agreement need not be reached on the "charged offense" alone. It may be made "to a lesser or related offense." See John Barkai, "Accuracy Inquiries for All Felony and Misdemeanor Pleas," 126 *U. Pa. L. Rev.* 88, 115 (1977) (noting that voluntariness "is constitutionally required in every jurisdiction for every category of crime" but that most states have no "accuracy requirement" for misdemeanors and some do not have it even for felonies. "The establishment of a factual basis can be more difficult, if not impossible, when the defendant pleads to a crime not encompassed in the original charge; consequently, some states do not require a factual basis for negotiated pleas" that may have been selected only because of their sentencing provisions).

18. McCarthy v. United States, 394 U.S., 466, 467. See *Notes of Advisory Committee* on *Federal Rules of Criminal Procedure*, Rule 11, 1966 Amendment; 18 U.S.C.A. (1975) and Supp. (1980); Comment, "Judicial Supervision over California Plea Bargaining: Regulating the Trade," 59 *Cal. L. Rev.* 962, 981 (1971) (The factual basis requirement "does not mean that the trial judge cannot accept the plea when he finds lack of sufficient correlation between the legal elements of the offense and the facts of the case before him. The factual basis examination is designed

to protect defendants from being induced or coerced into pleading to offenses that they could not have been convicted of at trial. If after proper notice defendant nevertheless wishes to convict himself, the court can accept the plea.").

19. State v. Gustafson, 214 N.W. 2d 341, 342 (Minn. 1974), (approving and quoting § 1.6 of the American Bar Association's *Standards Relating to Pleas of Guilty* [1968]).
20. 166 N.E. 2d 684 (N.Y. 1960).
21. The quotations are from 166 N.E. 2d, 686–87.
22. People v. Foster, 225 N.E. 2d 200, 203 (N.Y. 1967). See People v. Claiborne, 280 N.E. 2d 366, 367 (N.Y. 1962) ("a bargained guilty plea to a lesser crime makes unnecessary a factual basis for the particular crime confessed."). However, if a nonexistent crime is charged in the indictment itself, the defect is jurisdictional and cannot be waived by a guilty plea. The court treated a guilty plea to "attempted" felony murder as a guilty plea to "no crime" and distinguishable from *Foster*, in which "there was a plea of guilty to a lesser included crime of the higher crime charged in the indictment." People v. Hassin, 368 N.Y. Supp. 2d 253 (App. Div. 1975). "Only the events of time, place, and, if applicable, victim, need be the same for the crime pleaded as for the one charged." People v. Francis, 341 N.E. 2d 540, 543 (N.Y. 1975). Section 3.1 of the American Bar Association's *Standards Relating to Pleas of Guilty* (1968) seems to approve a procedure under which a defendant may plead to a hypothetical crime or to a crime he did not commit.
23. 400 U.S. 25 (1970). It should be noted that *Alford* permits, but does not require, the judge to accept the plea under such circumstances. Many trial judges are unwilling to do so because such pleas encourage a public perception that the plea has been coerced.
24. Bordenkircher v. Hayes, 434 U.S. 357, 364 (1978).
25. Smith v. State, 324 So. 2d 699 (Fla. App. 1976).
26. People v. West, 477 P.2d 409, 419–20 (Cal. 1970), adopting Section 3.1(b)(ii) of American Bar Association *Standards Relating to Pleas of Guilty* (1968), 68; Note, "Convictions of Unincluded Lesser Offenses: Informal Amendments and Plea Bargains," 25 *Hast. L. J.* 1075 (1974).
27. The embezzlement case is State v. Norris, 558 P.2d 903 (Ariz. 1976). The purse-snatching case is State v. McGhee, 551 P.2d 568 (Ariz. App. 1976). The first and third quotations are from *McGhee*, 551 P.2d, 571; the second is from *Norris*, 558 P.2d, 905.
28. People v. Clifton, 245 N.W. 2d 175 (Mich. App. 1976) (Where the two defendants were necessary parties to the commission of the offense of illegal delivery of drugs, an agreement between them cannot constitute separate crime of conspiracy, and a guilty plea to latter is in-

valid). See also Jones v. State, 505 S.W. 2d 903 (Tex. Cir. App. 1974) (a defendant may not plead *nolo contendre* to a charge that he was a principal when he was in fact only an accomplice).

29. People v. Johnson, 181 N.W. 2d 425, 429 (Mich. App. 1970).
30. People v. Burgan, 183 N.W. 2d 413, 414 (Mich. App. 1970). See also People ex rel Bassin v. Isreal, 335 N.E. 2d 53 (Ill. App. 1975) (holding that there may be a guilty plea to attempted voluntary manslaughter but suggesting that a plea to attempted involuntary manslaughter might be impermissible).
31. People v. Johnson, 181 N.W. 2d, 429.
32. State v. Staples, 354 A.2d 771, 780 (Me. 1976).
33. See Stephen J. Schulhofer, "Due Process of Sentencing", 128 *U. Pa. L. Rev.* 733 (1980); *id., Prosecutorial Discretion and Federal Sentencing Reform* (2 vols.; Washington, D.C.: Federal Judicial Center, 1979).
34. Newman, *Conviction*, 10, 233–35. See Alschuler, "The Trial Judge's Role in Plea Bargaining, Part I," 76 *Col. L. Rev.* at 1137–45.
35. See the several opinions in the California case of People v. Tanner, Chapter II, n.29.
36. Santobello v. New York, 404 U.S. 262 (1971); Lynch v. Overholser, 369 U.S. 705, 719 (1962); United States v. Bean, 564 F.2d 700, 703 (5th Cir. 1977); Maxwell v. United States, 368 F.2d 735, 738–39 (9th Cir. 1966). In McCoy v. United States, 363 F.2d 306, 307–8 (D.C. Cir. 1966), decided before *Alford*, the court "emphasize[d]" that the equivocal plea had been made to a lesser offense. "In that situation, a discretion remained with the trial court" to reject the plea, but only for a "good reason." The *Federal Rules of Criminal Procedure* confirmed that discretion by providing in Rule 11 that "the Court may refuse to accept a guilty plea." The current version of the rule omits that sentence and provides in a new section on plea agreements that "the court may accept or reject the agreement." The Notes of the Advisory Committee are silent on the effect of the change on a court's discretion to reject a plea which is not the result of a "plea agreement." However, by referring to the court's continuing authority to determine whether acceptance of an equivocal plea is consistent with "the interest of the public in the effective administration of justice," the Notes support the view that the judge retains his discretion to accept or reject a plea.
37. American Bar Association, *Standards Relating to Pleas of Guilty*, §§ 3.3(c) and 1.8 (1968). See also Comment, "Judicial Discretion to Reject Negotiated Pleas," 63 *Geo. L. .J.* 241, 250 (1974). The full text of § 1.8 of the ABA *Standards* follows:

(a) It is proper for the court to grant charge and sentence concessions to defendants who enter a plea of guilty or nolo contendere when the interest of the public in the effective administration of criminal justice would thereby be served. Among the considerations which are appropriate in determining this question are:

(i) that the defendant by his plea has aided in ensuring the prompt and certain application of correctional measures to him;

(ii) that the defendant has acknowledged his guilt and shown a willingness to assume responsibility for his conduct;

(iii) that the concessions will make possible alternative correctional measures which are better adapted to achieving rehabilitative, protective, deterrent or other purposes of correctional treatment, or will prevent undue harm to the defendant from the form of conviction;

(iv) that the defendant has made public trial unnecessary when there are good reasons for not having the case dealt with in a public trial;

(v) that the defendant has given or offered cooperation when such cooperation has resulted or may result in the successful prosecution of other offenders engaged in equally serious or more serious criminal conduct;

(vi) that the defendant by his plea has aided in avoiding delay (including delay due to crowded dockets) in the disposition of other cases and thereby has increased the probability of prompt and certain application of correctional measures to other offenders.

(b) The court should not impose upon a defendant any sentence in excess of that which would be justified by any of the rehabilitative, protective, deterrent or other purposes of the criminal law because the defendant has chosen to require the prosecution to prove his guilt at trial rather than to enter a plea of guilty or nolo contendere.

38. 40 P.2d 606, 607 (Colo. 1934).

39. 555 P.2d 269, 271–72 (Alaska, 1976) ("a trial court order directing the Attorney General to prosecute a case . . . violated the separation of powers because the decision whether to prosecute a case was committed to the discretion of the executive branch, and therefore was not subject to judicial control or review"). See also United States v. Gray, 448 F.2d 164, 168 (9th Cir. 1971) (plea to a lesser offense).

40. People ex rel Leonard v. Papp, 194 N.W. 2d 693, 699 (Mich. 1972).

41. Genesee County Prosecutor v. Genesee Circuit Judge, 215 N.W. 2d 145, 147 (Mich. 1974); People v. Curtis, 209 N.W. 2d 243, 249 (Mich. 1973).

42. 230 N.W. 2d 347, 351 (Mich. App. 1975). See also State v. Aubal, 244 N.W. 2d 636 (Minn. 1976) (appellate court reversed the trial judge's denial of prosecutor's motion to dismiss indictment on grounds of insufficiency of evidence—his showing conflicted with the evidence before the grand jury—saying that the judge may not substitute his judgment for that of the prosecutor unless he found "abuse of prosecutorial discretion [or] collusion [or] deceit").

43. 497 F.2d 615, 618 (D.C. Cir. 1973).

44. United States v. Ammidown, 497 F.2d, 619.

45. *Id.*, 621–23. And see United States v. Cowan, 524 F.2d, 513 (5th Cir. 1975).
46. United States v. Ammidown, 497 F.2d, 621, 624.
47. United States v. Maggio, 514 F.2d 80, 90 (5th Cir. 1975), cert. den. 423 U.S. 1032 (1975) (defendant has "a conditional right to have his guilty plea accepted. . . . [The] district court may not issue a blanket proscription of plea agreements of the kind where the prosecution drops some charges in exchange for the defendant's guilty plea to other charges." The court's role is "secondary and complementary to that of the prosecutor").
48. United States v. Bean, 564 F.2d, 703.
49. James W. Moore, *Federal Practice* (2nd ed.; 12 vols.; Albany: Matthew Bender, 1979), VIII, § 11.02 (1) (1979).

III.

1. Department of Justice, *Principles of Federal Prosecution* (July, 1980), rpr. in 27 *Cr. L.* 3277–92 (Aug. 6, 1980). See American Law Institute, *A Model Code of Pre-Arraignment Procedure* (1975), § 350.3(2) 613–14; American Bar Association, *Standards Relating to the Prosecution Function and the Defense Function* (1971), § 2.5; Kenneth C. Davis, *Discretionary Justice: A Preliminary Inquiry* (Baton Rouge: Louisiana State University Press, 1969), 224–25; Norman Abrams, "Internal Policy: Guiding the Exercise of Prosecutorial Discretion," 19 *U.C.L.A.* 1 (1971).
2. See *The Federalist Papers*, ed. Clinton Rossiter (New York: New American Library, 1961), No. 48, 308–11 (No. 48 was written by James Madison). "The Madisonian conception is now generally accepted in the United States." Note, "The Proposed Court-Appointed Special Prosecutor, 87 *Yale L. J.* 1692 (1978) (citing United States v. Nixon, 418 U.S. 683, 707 [1974] and Jackson, J., concurring in Youngstown Sheet & Tube Co. v. Sawyer, 343 U.S. 579, 635 [1952]). See generally Malcolm P. Sharp, "The Classical American Doctrine of 'The Separation of Powers,'" 2 *U. Chi. L. Rev.* 385 (1935); Benjamin F. Wright, "The Origins of the Separation of Powers in America," *Economica* (May, 1933), 169; Geoffrey Marshall, *Constitutional Theory* 100 (Oxford: Clarendon Press, 1971); Robert G. Dixon, Jr., "The Doctrine of Separation of Powers and Federal Immunity Statutes," 23 *Geo. Wash. L. Rev.* 501, 627 (1955).
3. United States v. Ammidown, 497 F.2d, 622.
4. United States v. Cowan, 524 F.2d, 512.
5. Nader v. Saxbe, 497 F.2d, 679–80 n.19 (D.C. Cir. 1974).

6. See, *e.g.*, Inmates of Attica Correctional Facility v. Rockefeller, 477 F.2d 375, 379–82 (2nd Cir. 1973), in which the court concluded that even if there were standing, the complaint was insufficient because the United States attorney and the state prosecutors had an unreviewable discretion to prosecute or not. The court based its conclusion on "the separation of powers" doctrine:

> In the absence of statutorily defined standards governing reviewability, or regulatory or statutory policies of prosecution, the problems inherent in the task of supervising prosecutorial decisions do not lend themselves to resolution by the judiciary. The reviewing courts would be placed in the undesirable and injudicious posture of becoming 'super-prosecutors.' In the normal case of review of executive acts of discretion, the administrative record is open, public and reviewable on the basis of what it contains. The decision not to prosecute, on the other hand, may be based upon the insufficiency of the available evidence, in which event the secrecy of the grand jury and of the prosecutor's file may serve to protect the accused's reputation from public damage based upon insufficient, improper, or even malicious charges. In camera review would not be meaningful without access by the complaining party to the evidence before the grand jury or U.S. Attorney. . . . Nor is it clear what the judiciary's role of supervision should be were it to undertake such a review. At what point would the prosecutor be entitled to call a halt to further investigation as unlikely to be productive? What evidentiary standard would be used to decide whether prosecution should be compelled? How much judgment would the United States Attorney be allowed? Would he be permitted to limit himself to a strong test case rather than pursue weaker cases? What collateral factors would be permissible bases for a decision not to prosecute, e.g., the pendency of another criminal proceeding elsewhere against the same parties? . . . What sort of review should be available in cases like the present one where the conduct complained of allegedly violates state as well as federal laws? . . . With limited personnel and facilities at his disposal, what priority would the prosecutor be required to give to cases in which investigation or prosecution was directed by the court?
>
> These difficult questions engender serious doubts as to the judiciary's capacity to review and as to the problem of arbitrariness inherent in any judicial decision to order prosecution. On balance, we believe that substitution of a court's decision to compel prosecution for the U.S. Attorney's decision not to prosecute, even upon an abuse of discretion standard of review and even if limited to directing that a prosecution be undertaken in good faith . . . would be unwise.

7. 359 F.2d 234 (D.C. Cir. 1965).
8. See Chap. 1, note 40, herein. An unusual illustration of the blending of powers exists in Connecticut, where prosecutors are appointed by judges. In that state, investigation of crime has always been under judi-

cial control, not only when the regular grand jury is used but through the so-called one-man jury. State v. Moynahan, 325 A.2d 199 (Conn. 1973), cert. den. 414 U.S. 976 (1973).

9. The quotation is from Newman v. United States, 382 F.2d 479, 480 (D.C. Cir. 1967) (involving dismissal of the higher offense originally charged and a plea agreement to a lesser offense.)

10. Charles A. Wright, *Federal Practice and Procedure* (3 vols.; St. Paul, Minn.: West, 1974), III, § 812, p. 305; *Uniform Rules of Criminal Procedure* (St. Paul, Minn.: West, 1957), Comment on Rule 231(h), 52. United States v. Greater Blouse, Skirt & Neckwear Contractors Association 228 F.Supp. 489 (S.D.N.Y. 1964).

11. Of course, it is not always so simple. Though the defendant's statements in the course of plea discussions may not be used against him, others may have been charged or convicted on the basis of his disclosures. There are surprisingly few cases dealing with the question whether such charges or convictions could be unraveled or set aside as a result of the denial of the motion to dismiss or rejection of the plea bargain. It is doubtful that third parties affected by the disclosures would benefit from application to them of a "fruit of the poisoned tree" doctrine. See Wong Sun v. United States, 371 U.S. 471 (1962).

12. The first quotation is from Herbert L. Packer, *The Limits of the Criminal Sanction* (Stanford: Stanford University Press, 1968), 290 ("The basic trouble with discretion is simply that it is lawless"). See also Arthur Rosett, "Discretion, Severity and Legality in Criminal Justice," 46 *So. Cal. L. Rev.* 12, 15 (1972) (equating discretion with "normlessness, the absence of controlling substantive standards," which is most likely to exist in informal processes that provide "opportunities for uncontrolled deviation from the governing norm"). The second quotation is from Davis, *Discretionary Justice* 4, who notes that "a good deal of discretion is illegal." See Ronald M. Dworkin, "The Model of Rules," 35 *U. Chi. L. Rev.* 14, 32–33 (1967), which collects the several meanings of discretion—*e.g.*, "the standards an official must apply cannot be applied mechanically but demand the use of judgment . . . [or] that some official has final authority to make a decision and cannot be reviewed and reversed by any other official . . . [or] that on some issue he is simply not bound by the authority in question."

13. Mortimer Kadish and Sanford Kadish, *Discretion to Disobey: A Study of Lawful Departures from Legal Rules* (Stanford: Stanford University Press, 1973).

14. See George P. Fletcher, "The Ideology of Prosecutorial Discretion" (Unpublished paper delivered at Yale Law School, Feb. 26, 1975).

15. Prosecutors were "invariably unaware of information that even a rou-

tine pre-sentence investigation would have uncovered." Albert W. Alschuler, "The Trial Judge's Role in Plea Bargaining, Part I.," 76 *Col. L. Rev.* 1059, 1063 (1976).

16. William M. Rhodes, "Plea Bargaining: Its Effect on Sentencing and Convictions in the District of Columbia," 70 *J. Crim. L. & Crimin.* 360, 375 (1979). On the tension between the "real" offense and the guilty plea, particularly in the context of charge reduction, see Stephen J. Schulhofer, "Due Process of Sentencing," 128 *U. Pa. L. Rev.* 733 (1980).
17. See recommendation of American Bar Association, *Standards Relating to Pleas of Guilty* (1968), § 3.1(c), discussed in Donald J. Newman, "The Agnew Plea Bargain," 10 *Crim. L. Bull.* 85, 88 (1974).
18. People v. Mack, 125 Cal. Rptr. 188, 191 (App. 2nd Dist. 1975). See cases cited in Chap. 1, note 41, herein, holding that judicial dismissal on such grounds in the federal courts must have the consent of the prosecutor.
19. See the proposal for abolition of negotiation for "concessions to be made in return for guilty pleas," which argues that it would "eliminate the incentive for prosecutors to overcharge or inappropriately charge." National Advisory Commission on Criminal Justice Standards and Goals, *The Courts* (Washington, D.C.: Government Printing Office, 1974), 46–47; Michael L. Rubinstein, Stevens H. Clarke, and Teresa J. White, *The Effect of the Official Prohibition of Plea Bargaining on the Disposition of Felony Cases in Alaska Criminal Courts* (Anchorage: Alaska Judicial Council, 1979), 223–24 ("Plea bargaining had never been primarily responsible for the Alaska criminal justice system's heavy dependence upon dismissals and admissions of guilt. . . . Most guilty pleas and dismissals were entered because the parties simply did not perceive any better alternatives. . . . With or without plea bargaining, guilty pleas continued at the same rate."); James Vorenberg, "Narrowing the Discretion of Criminal Justice Officials," 1976 *Duke L. J.* 651, 671, 680 (1976). Compare Thomas Church, "Plea Bargains, Concessions and the Courts: Analysis of a Quasi-Experiment," 10 *Law & Soc. Rev.* 377 (1976) (who argues that concessions—by either the prosecutor or the judge—are essential to a high volume of guilty pleas) with Raymond I. Parnas and Riley J. Atkins, "Abolishing Plea Bargaining: A Proposal," 14 *Cr. L. Bull.* 101 (1978). For an interesting discussion of the view that "under supportive conditions, negotiation can be a source of greater rationality in the administration of criminal justice, and a more genuine fidelity to law," see Pamela Utz, *Settling the Facts: Discretion and Negotiation in Criminal Court* (Lexington, Mass.: Lexington Books, 1978), Chap. 13.
20. Another reason sometimes offered for limiting judicial review of the

prosecutor is that, as an elected official, he is closer to the people than the judge and can be turned out of office if he is not doing the people's bidding in enforcing the criminal law. This begs the question. Judges, too, are sometimes elected officials in the states where prosecutors are elected. Moreover, much the same body of law governs in places where prosecutors are elected and where they are appointed.

21. Compare the experience in several European countries that place much more explicit reliance on judicial initiative. In an article in 1974, I suggested that it might be useful to look to such systems for guidance in these matters of prosecutorial discretion and guilty pleas. Abraham S. Goldstein, "Reflections on Two Models: Inquisitorial Themes in American Criminal Procedure," 26 *Stan. L. Rev.* 1009, 1025 (1974). In a subsequent article based in part on interviews abroad, we called attention to the degree to which judges in those systems, too, tend to be passive in relation to police and prosecutors, and cautioned against uncritical use of foreign models. Abraham S. Goldstein and Martin Marcus, "The Myth of Judicial Supervision in Three Inquisitorial Systems: France, Italy, and Germany," 87 *Yale L. J.* 240 (1977). These views evoked strong disagreement from John H. Langbein and Lloyd Weinreb, "Continental Criminal Procedure: 'Myth' and Reality," 87 *Yale L. J.* 1549 (1978). For our reply, see Abraham S. Goldstein and Martin Marcus, "Comment on Continental Criminal Procedure," 87 *Yale L. J.* 1570 (1978).
22. See the discussion of these matters in Davis, *Discretionary Justice*, 219–26.
23. See William F. McDonald, "Towards a Bicentennial Revolution in Criminal Justice: The Return of the Victim," 13 *Am. Crim. L. Rev.* 649 (1976); Donald J. Hall, "The Role of the Victim in the Prosecution and Disposition of a Criminal Case," 28 *Vand. L. Rev.* 931 (1975); Note, "Private Prosecution: A Remedy for District Attorney's Unwarranted Inaction," 65 *Yale L. J.* 209 (1955).
24. Vera Institute of Justice, *Felony Arrests: Their Prosecution and Disposition in New York City's Courts* (New York: 1977), 135–40.
25. It would, of course, be desirable to have the victim's right to participate defined by statute or rule. But the courts could arguably confer the requisite "standing" themselves, in aid of the "sound discretion" they are required to exercise on these matters. This "standing" would be based either on the relation between the victim's injury and the public "cause of action" or on his position as a "private attorney general" who is especially well situated to vindicate the public interest in criminal law.

The initial charging decision falls into another and more inviolate category. But it is insulated only from judicial intervention. There is nothing to prevent the prosecutor from routinely inviting the victim (and his counsel) to a precharge conference and soliciting his views on what the charge should be.

26. Davis, *Discretionary Justice*, Chap. 7.

27. See Rosett, "Discretion, Severity and Legality in Criminal Justice," 46 *So. Cal. L. Rev.* at 30 et seq.; Compare Norval Morris, "Book Review," 91 *Harv. L. Rev.* 1367, 1370 (1978) (discussing the development of explicit sentencing discounts for those who plead guilty) with Stephen J. Schulhofer, *Prosecutorial Discretion and Federal Sentencing Reform*, I, 63 (urging rejection of a declared policy of placing greater weight in sentencing on the judge's conception of "offense behavior than upon the formal offense of conviction. . . . It is hard to imagine a more striking way for the legal system to proclaim its mistrust of its own processes").

INDEX

Accuracy of pleas, 34, 40, 43–47, 92*n*22
Attorney general of England, 12

Bordenkircher v. *Hayes*, 37, 43
Brady v. *United States*, 35

Cardozo, Judge Benjamin N., 27
Charging power: discretionary prosecution, 9, 11; discriminatory prosecution, 10, 62, 80*n*7; limited by norms of equality, 11; reduction of charges, 24; sentencing power, effect on, 61
Common law: prosecutorial discretion, 52
Commonwealth v. *Wheeler*, 12
Confiscation cases, 12
Coolidge v. *New Hampshire*, 7
Correctional considerations, 60–62
County attorney. *See* Prosecutor
Criminal justice systems: federal and state, compared, 4, 69, 77*n*2; inquisitorial v. accusatorial, 4, 77*n*3
Criminal law: nonenforcement of, 5, 9, 63

Diversion from prosecution, 24
Discretion: executive prerogative, 23, 58; judicial, 18, 23, 47; nature of, 57–58; oppressive use of, 13; to prosecute, 9, 11, 80*n*7. *See also* Prosecutorial discretion
Discriminatory prosecution, 10, 62–64
Dismissal of charge: denial of motion to dismiss, 21, 84*n*41; judicial discretion, 16, 18, 23, 84*n*41; judicial power, 13, 16, 24, 62, 82*n*24, 84*n*41; law of, summarized, 24; why requested, 58, 83*n*34, 83*n*36; workload reduction, 64; mentioned, 12
District attorney. *See* Prosecutor
Doyle v. *Hofstadter*, 27

Enforcement policy, 63
England: private prosecution, 4; *nolle prosequi*, 12
Equal treatment for offenders, 11, 62
Exclusionary rule, 5, 78*n*4
Evidence: sufficiency of, 59

Failure to prosecute, 5, 9, 56, 59, 63, 79*n*4
Federal Rules of Criminal Procedure: 11(e), plea bargaining, 38, 43, 90*n*14; 11(f), accuracy of plea, 41, 93*n*36; 16(b), discovery procedure exclusions, 80*n*11; 48(a),

dismissal authority, 17, 84*n*41
Frady v. *People*, 47

Gemmill, Judge William, 13
Gerstein v. *Pugh*, 7
Guilty plea: accuracy of, 34, 40–41, 43–47, 88*n*1, 92*n*22; defendant understanding, 39; exposing facts behind plea, 34, 40, 88*n*1, 91*n*16; involuntary, 37, 89*n*7; judicial discretion, 47; judicial role, 35, 40, 45, 93*n*37; negotiated, 33; public interest in, 33, 45; real v. legal offense, 44–45, 100*n*27; research relating to, 58; sentencing power, 66; standards, American Bar Association, 93*n*37; structurally induced, 33, 37; threats in procuring, 38; voluntary, 33, 39, 47, 90*n*14. *See also* Plea bargaining
Grand jury, 21

Hincks, Judge Carroll, 18

Immunity from prosecution: coupled with formal charge, 31; history and present status, 25; informal procedures, 26, 31, 88*n*59; judicial function relating to, 25, 27–32, 64; Model State Witness Immunity Act, 25, 69, 86*n*46; separation of powers doctrine, effect, 31; statutory procedures, 25–26, 31
Inmates of Attica Correctional Facility v. *Rockefeller*, 96*n*6

Judicial passivity and initiative, 6, 57, 67–70
Judicial power and discretion: California experience, 14–16; charge dismissal, 14, 17, 23, 54, 82*n*24, 83*n*34, 84*n*41; compelling prosecution, 13, 20, 56, 62; European experience, 99*n*21; inability to enforce decisions, 20, 55, 56; legislative grants of power, 14; offenders, equal treatment of, 62; state v. federal system, 69; undermining authority of judges, 53
Judicial review: accuracy of pleas, 45, 60, 93*n*36; choice among conflicting statutes, 60; dismissals, 4, 12, 14, 20, 23, 54, 82*n*24, 83*n*34, 84*n*41; evidence, sufficiency of, 59; guilty pleas, 4, 34–35, 47, 54, 88*n*1, 93*n*36; immunity, grants of, 25, 31, 54; lesser charge, rejection of, 46; plea bargain, rejection of, 46, 48, 93*n*36; prosecutor accountability, 4, 6, 74; prosecutorial discretion, 4, 51; prosecutor's file, 68; separation of powers doctrine, 53, 54, 96*n*6; standards of review, 48–51, 53

Kadish, Mortimer, and Sanford, 58

Legality and discretion, 5–6, 10, 57–58
Linda R.S. v. *Richard D.*, 9, 79*n*4

Model State Witness Immunity Act, 25, 69, 86*n*46

Nolle prosequi, writ of: California experience, 14–17; history and present status, 12–14, 20, 54, 81*n*12; judicial control of, and use, 14, 16; judicial review, limitations on, 12, 20
North Carolina v. *Alford*, 36, 43

Offenders: equal treatment of, 11, 62
Offense: relation of, to plea, 40, 43, 46, 92*n*22
Oyler v. *Boles*, 10, 80*n*7

People v. *Brunner*, 28
People v. *Griffin*, 41

People v. *Matulonis*, 48
People v. *Tanner*, 16
Plea bargaining: abolishing, 67, 98*n*19; *Federal Rules of Criminal Procedure*, 38, 41, 90*n*14; hypothetical or inconsistent pleas, 41; judicial rejection and its effect, 47–51, 57, 93*n*36, 97*n*11; legitimation by Supreme Court, 34–38; reducing charges, reasons for, 41, 58, 64; threats, 37, 90*n*14; when facts and law contested, 67. *See also* Guilty plea
Plea discussions *v.* plea bargains, 67, 98*n*19
Pound, Roscoe, 13–14
Powell v. *Katzenbach*, 54
Prior conviction: "striking the priors," 15
Prosecution, private, 4, 12
Prosecutor: as administrative official, 6, 78*n*9; access to files of, 11, 80*n*11. *See also* Special prosecutor
—appointment or election: federal system, 4; state systems, 4, 77*n*2
—role of: administrative official, 6, 78*n*9; charging authority, 9, 73, 80*n*7; conflicting roles, 6, 9, 78*n*8; dismissals, *nolle prosequi*, 12; executive role, 5, 23, 55–56, 57, 96*n*6; independence, 4; judicial function regarding role, 4, 47, 51, 54–55, 57, 74–75; partisan nature of role, 7; plea bargaining, 33, 37, 39, 47, 90*n*14; *Principles of Prosecution*, 52; sentencing, influence of role on, 66; mentioned, 3
Prosecutorial discretion: developing a common law of, 52; elimination of, 54; evidence, sufficiency of, 59; failure to prosecute, 5, 9, 56, 59, 63, 79*n*4; immunity, conferring of, 25–30; initiation of charge, 4, 54, 56, 74; obligation to prosecute, 9; reform, 52; standards for, 52, 97*n*12; statutes, choice among conflicting charges, 60; undermining judicial authority, 53, 60. *See also* Judicial review
Public interest: court's role in defining, 6, 17, 19, 20, 23, 34, 60, 63, 74

Reduced charge: reasons for requesting, 58, 65

Santobello v. *New York*, 30, 36, 88*n*59
Self-incrimination and immunity, 25
Sentencing power: affected by charge, 61; court function as to, 53, 66
Separation of powers doctrine, 5, 16, 19, 23, 24, 51, 53–58, 69, 83*n*40, 96*n*6
Special prosecutor, 22–23, 24, 83*n*40
Standing, 4, 9, 79*n*4
State v. *Carlson*, 47
State v. *Wynne*, 63
State's attorney. *See* Prosecutor
Statute: choice of, in charging, 60

Uniform Rules of Criminal Procedure, 20, 56, 83*n*36
United States v. *Ammidown*, 48
United States v. *Carter*, 29
United States v. *Cowan*, 22
United States v. *Cox*, 21
United States v. *Doe*, 18
United States v. *Falk*, 11
United States v. *Greater Blouse . . . Association*, 19
United States v. *Shanahan*, 18

Victims of crime: and adversary process, 70–71; stake in prosecution, 71, 72–73; standing to compel prosecution, 4, 9, 79*n*4,

99*n*25; varied nature of, 71–72
Voluntary pleas: public interest in, 40

Warrants, arrest and search, 32
Weinfeld, Judge Edward, 10
Whiskey cases, 27
Wright, Charles Allen, 20, 56, 83*n*36

Yick Wo v. *Hopkins*, 10
Young v. *United States*, 5